THE GREEK TRAGEDY
IN NEW TRANSLATIONS

GENERAL EDITOR   William Arrowsmith

CO-EDITOR   Herbert Golder

SOPHOCLES: Oedipus the King

SOPHOCLES

Oedipus the King

Translated by
STEPHEN BERG

and
DISKIN CLAY

OXFORD UNIVERSITY PRESS
New York

Oxford University Press

Oxford   New York   Toronto
Delhi   Bombay   Calcutta   Madras   Karachi
Petaling Jaya   Singapore   Hong Kong   Tokyo
Nairobi   Dar es Salaam   Cape Town
Melbourne   Auckland

and associated companies in
Beirut   Berlin   Ibadan   Nicosia

First published in 1978 by Oxford University Press, Inc.,
198 Madison Avenue, New York, New York 10016-4314

First issued as an Oxford University Press paperback, 1988

Oxford is a registered trademark of Oxford University Press

Lines 1502–1572 first appeared in *Contemporary Literature in Translation*,
edited by Robert Bringhurst.

I am grateful to the John Simon Guggenheim Memorial Foundation
for a fellowship which gave me the time to do much of the work
on this translation.   STEPHEN BERG

To William Arrowsmith

Library of Congress Cataloging in Publication Data

Sophocles.
Oedpius the king.
(The Greek tragedy in new translations)
Translation of Oedipus tyrannus.
Includes bibliographical references.
I. Berg, Stephen   II. Clay, Diskin.   III. Title.
PA4414.07B44   882'.01   77-10964
ISBN 0-19-502325-0
ISBN 0-19-505493-8 (PPBK)

20 19 18 17 16 15 14 13 12

Printed in the United States of America

EDITOR'S FOREWORD

The Greek Tragedy in New Translations is based on the conviction that poets like Aeschylus, Sophocles, and Euripides can only be properly rendered by translators who are themselves poets. Scholars may, it is true, produce useful and perceptive versions. But our most urgent present need is for a re-creation of these plays—as though they had been written, freshly and greatly, by masters fully at home in the English of our own times. Unless the translator is a poet, his original is likely to reach us in crippled form: deprived of the power and pertinence it must have if it is to speak to us of what is permanent in the Greek. But poetry is not enough; the translator must obviously know what he is doing, or he is bound to do it badly. Clearly, few contemporary poets possess enough Greek to undertake the complex and formidable task of transplanting a Greek play without also "colonializing" it or stripping it of its deep cultural difference, its remoteness from us. And that means depriving the play of that crucial otherness of Greek experience—a quality no less valuable to us than its closeness. Collaboration between scholar and poet is therefore the essential operating principle of the series. In fortunate cases scholar and poet co-exist; elsewhere we have teamed able poets and scholars in an effort to supply, through affinity and intimate collaboration, the necessary combination of skills.

An effort has been made to provide the general reader or student with first-rate critical introductions, clear expositions of translators' principles, commentary on difficult passages, ample stage directions, and glossaries of mythical and geographical terms encountered in the plays. Our purpose throughout has been to make the reading of the plays as vivid as possible. But our poets have constantly tried to remember that they were translating *plays*—plays meant to be produced, in language that actors could speak, naturally and with dignity. The poetry aims at being *dramatic* poetry and realizing itself in words and actions that are both speakable and playable.

Finally, the reader should perhaps be aware that no pains have been spared in order that the "minor" plays should be translated as carefully and brilliantly as the acknowledged masterpieces. For the Greek Tragedy in New Translations aims to be, in the fullest sense, *new*. If we need vigorous new poetic versions, we also need to see the plays with fresh eyes, to reassess the plays *for ourselves*, in terms of our own needs. This means translations that liberate us from the canons of an earlier age because the translators have recognized, and discovered, in often neglected works, the perceptions and wisdom that make these works ours and necessary to us.

A NOTE ON THE SERIES FORMAT

If only for the illusion of coherence, a series of thirty-three Greek plays requires a consistent format. Different translators, each with his individual voice, cannot possibly develop the sense of a single coherent style for each of the three tragedians; nor even the illusion that, despite their differences, the tragedians share a common set of conventions and a generic, or period, style. But they can at least share a common approach to orthography and a common vocabulary of conventions.

1. *Spelling of Greek Names*

Adherence to the old convention whereby Greek names were first Latinized before being housed in English is gradually disappearing. We are now clearly moving away from Latinization and toward precise transliteration. The break with tradition may be regrettable, but there is much to be said for hearing and seeing Greek names as though they were both *Greek* and *new*, instead of Roman or neo-classical importations. We cannot of course see them as wholly new. For better or worse certain names and myths are too deeply rooted in our literature and thought to be dislodged. To speak of "Helene" and "Hekabe" would be no less pedantic and absurd than to write "Aischylos" or "Platon" or "Thoukydides." There are of course borderline cases. "Jocasta" (as opposed to "Iokaste") is not a major mythical figure in her own right; her familiarity in her Latin form is a function of the fame of Sophocles' play as the tragedy *par excellence*. And as tourists we go to Delphi, not Delphoi. The precisely transliterated form may be pedantically "right," but the pedantry goes against the grain of cultural habit and actual usage.

As a general rule, we have therefore adopted a "mixed" orthography according to the principles suggested above. When a name has been firmly housed in English (admittedly the question of domestication is often moot), the traditional spelling has been kept. Otherwise names have been transliterated. Throughout the series the -os termination of masculine names has been adopted, and Greek diphthongs (as in Iphigeneia) have normally been retained. We cannot expect complete agreement from readers (or from translators, for that matter) about borderline cases. But we want at least to make the operative principle clear: to walk a narrow line between orthographical extremes in the hope of keeping what should not, if possible, be lost; and refreshing, in however tenuous a way, the specific sound and name-boundedness of Greek experience.

2. *Stage directions*

The ancient manuscripts of the Greek plays do not supply stage directions (though the ancient commentators often provide information relevant to staging, delivery, "blocking," etc.). Hence stage directions must be inferred from words and situations and our knowledge of Greek theatrical conventions. At best this is a ticklish and uncertain procedure. But it is surely preferable that good stage directions should be provided by the translator than that the reader should be left to his own devices in visualizing action, gesture, and spectacle. Obviously the directions supplied should be both spare and defensible. Ancient tragedy was austere and "distanced" by means of masks, which means that the reader must not expect the detailed intimacy ("He shrugs and turns wearily away," "She speaks with deliberate slowness, as though to emphasize the point," etc.) which characterizes stage directions in modern naturalistic drama. Because Greek drama is highly rhetorical and stylized, the translator knows that his words must do the real work of inflection and nuance. Therefore every effort has been made to supply the visual and tonal sense required by a given scene and the reader's (or actor's) putative unfamiliarity with the ancient conventions.

3. *Numbering of lines.*

For the convenience of the reader who may wish to check the English against the Greek text or vice versa, the lines have been numbered according to both the Greek text and the translation. The lines of the English translation have been numbered in multiples of ten, and these numbers have been set in the right-hand margin. The (inclusive) Greek numeration will be found bracketed at the top of the page. The reader will doubtless note that in many plays the English lines outnumber the Greek, but he should not therefore conclude that the translator has been unduly prolix. In most cases the reason is simply that the translator has adopted the free-flowing norms of modern Anglo-American prosody, with its brief, breath- and emphasis-determined lines, and its habit of indicating cadence and caesuras by line length and setting rather than by conventional punctuation. Other translators have preferred four-beat or five-beat lines, and in these cases Greek and English numerations will tend to converge.

4. Notes and Glossary

In addition to the Introduction, each play has been supplemented by Notes (identified by the line numbers of the translation) and a Glossary. The Notes are meant to supply information which the translators deem important to the interpretation of a passage; they also afford the translator an opportunity to justify what he has done. The Glossary is intended to spare the reader the trouble of going elsewhere to look up mythical or geographical terms. The entries are not meant to be comprehensive; when a fuller explanation is needed, it will be found in the Notes.

ABOUT THE TRANSLATION

This new translation of Sophocles' masterpiece *Oedipus the King* is the product of several years of close and intense collaboration by one of America's most talented poets with a young classical scholar of exceptional achievement and future promise.

Stephen Berg is the author of four books of poetry: *Bearing Weapons* (1963), *The Queen's Triangle* (1969), and, more recently, *The Daughters* (1971) and *Grief* (1975), acclaimed as one of the finer books of poetry by an American poet in the seventies. He has also done translations of Aztec poetry (*Nothing in the Word*) and, with Stephen Polgar and S. J. Marks, a translation of the Hungarian Miklos Radnoti's *Clouded Sky*. In 1970 Berg was awarded the Frank O'Hara Prize for poems published in *Poetry* and, in 1974, a Guggenheim Fellowship for Poetry. He is also an editor, as well as a founder, of the *American Poetry Review*. His scholar-collaborator, Professor

Diskin Clay, is chairman of the Department of Classics at The Johns
Hopkins University. A discerning student of Greek poetry and philos-
ophy and their complex interrelationship, he is the author of a major
study of Lucretius and Epicurus, to be published in 1978. Finally, he
is himself a practising poet whose first book, Oxyrhynchan Poems, was
published in 1973.

To my perhaps prejudiced eye, the special achievements of this
new translation of Oedipus the King are, first, the functional precision
and power of its poetry; and, second, its pervasive metaphysical sug-
gestiveness. Again and again the play, but also the translation, evokes
the sense of another, larger world, of an eternally recurring reality
looming behind, sometimes violently erupting into, the immediate
foreground, here and now, of the dramatic situation. The concrete
human darkness is everywhere created and felt—the labyrinthine
world of the human condition. But because we feel the maze, we
also feel the sudden, blinding relief of the illusory exit, as darkness is
resolved into light which turns into hopeless darkness again. Beyond
this world the poet makes us always aware of what, to the Greek
dramatist and his audience, mattered even more—the generic modal
reality, the archetypal world which informs and finally patterns the
immediate world of real characters in a real but transient present. At
their greatest, it was the supreme achievement of the Greek drama-
tists to make, as Dante did later, a single seamless reality of these two
worlds. Inexorably, the timeless world of the "background" fills out,
and reveals, the permanent meaning of the present, just as the present
reaches out for, and finally achieves, eternity. Time, in Shakespeare's
great figure, makes stale "the glistering of this present" but also
renews it as an image of the endlessly recurring design.

So, if we respond to the poet's intentions, we see, not some existen-
tial identity-quest (though that is there), or some Christian passion-
play of crime-and-punishment (which is not there), but the great
concrete shadow-play of the species itself. We see how Oedipus, self-
sufficient and strong, godlike in his confidence of mother-wit and
power and self-reliance, in the space of one brief symbolic day is trans-
formed into the old, blind, decrepit but clairvoyant pariah-prophet
of his own riddle; and we see too how, as Oedipus passes from the
scene, like a setting sun, he is in turn succeeded by a new man of
power—a man called, with telling effect, simply Kreon (which in
Greek means merely "ruler" or "king"). We see, theatrically, how the
Chorus's great dirge on human transience is acted out in real and

metaphysical time:

man after man after man
o mortal generations
here once
almost not here
what are we
dust ghosts images a rustling of air
nothing nothing
we breathe on the abyss
we are the abyss
our happiness no more than the traces of a dream
the high noon sun sinking into the sea
the red spume of its wake raining behind it
we are you
we are you Oedipus

In the terrible sockets of Oedipus' mask we may even be tempted to see "the skull beneath the skin" and the transience of the body's glory, draped at first in cloth of gold, then in cerements of blood.

We may also come to see what I think the poet intends Oedipus' tragedy to reveal—the revelation of the god Apollo, and Apollo's presence in the hero's *pathos*. For a Greek god is not, as too many moderns suppose, some sort of deified function or capacity, or power of nature. Apollo, for instance, is not simply a god of reason. Not unless one possesses, as the Greeks did, a sense of reason so ample that discursive logic, lyric poetry, music, and prophecy—but above all prophecy—are, all of them, wholly rational activities, i.e. activities of the whole mind, thought literally fused with feeling. Nor is Apollo in any real sense a god of light, but rather a light-bringer, a god whose quality is the radiance he confers. A Greek god is experienced; his name is the name of that experience. Whenever we feel our mortal darkness illuminated; whenever we feel sudden clarity stabbing into our darkness—as when we are literally *enlightened* by poetry, or music, or logic, or prophecy, or insight—then Apollo is the name of what has happened to us. In this play Oedipus is the vehicle—both victim and hero—of this illumination. In his terrible darkness he comes to know the god and even, like Teiresias or the old hero of the *Oedipus at Kolonos*, to incarnate, even to be, the god. The hero's life is that of all men, rising and shining, then fading and falling. But their life is also the life of the god, daily rising and daily setting. The play's symbolic day—dawn to dusk—is in fact Apollo appearing, as he appears to all, before daily disappearing. The day reveals the man, the hero, the god.

Apollo and Oedipus, we may assume at first, are at odds. But one of the effects of the play as it unfolds is to reveal the affinity between the god and Oedipus. True, the affinity is never stated, only hinted. But we will misread the play, I believe, unless we are prepared to hear in Oedipus' insistence that he did not destroy himself because he was being preserved for some fate more awful, more dreadful still, the hero's fierce pride in having been *chosen* for a fate that would have broken a lesser man. It is an *extraordinary* fate, a doom which could have befallen no ordinary man. And Oedipus' sense of election by the god is reflected in his pride of having been doomed to so exceptional a fate. In some very real sense Oedipus knows that he is Apollo's man. The god moves in him, blazes in him, as he does in Teiresias too. And the course of Oedipus' life incarnates the god's, as well as revealing the god's power and, paradoxically, his justice—the justice of tragic life itself—to those who have eyes to see with, and the wit to be blinded by what they see.

Baltimore, Maryland   William Arrowsmith

CONTENTS

OEDIPUS THE KING

INTRODUCTION

I

The first thing we know about Oedipus is what we see. Fixed, king-like, powerful, his features do not change. His face is a mask. Oedipus' first words, and the very fact that he has appeared in person to meet a delegation of Thebans, show that he is a man of compassion. Thebes is not at three removes from its king. When Kreon arrives with news from Delphi, he asks Oedipus if he does not prefer to go inside the palace to hear Apollo's response. Oedipus would rather hear the response "with all these people listening." The action of the *Oedipus* begins in the open, and Oedipus is onstage throughout the play. Even when he is in the palace and out of sight, he remains within the range of the choral song and at the center of the speech of the palace serv-ant who comes out to report Jocasta's death and Oedipus' self-blinding. When Oedipus last appears before the Chorus and the audi-ence in the theater of Dionysos, his mask and its great hollow eyes are bloodstained.

"Children, why are you here?" Oedipus asks this question, but he already knows its answer, and he has been quick to act on what he knows. While the people of Thebes crowd the temples and shrines of the city's gods and look into embers for signs of their disposition (27-28), Oedipus has not been asleep. Confronted with the plague that is wasting his city, he has already attempted to work from effect to cause, and has sent to Delphi and the oracle of Apollo for a re-sponse to his question: "What must *I* say or do to save Thebes?" At the beginning of the *Oedipus*, Oedipus is both ahead of the action of the play and behind it.

The *Oedipus* begins with a question, and in no other Greek tragedy are more questions asked. As Oedipus attempts to discern the unknown in the physiognomy of the known, one question inevitably leads to another. Oedipus has experience. This is why the delegation of Thebans turn to him in their quest for a better future. They hope that the past will be a guide to this future and know that Oedipus' intelligence has already been tested in his encounter with the Sphinx (53-58). When Kreon arrives on stage, Oedipus prays for good luck and the safety Kreon's face seems to promise (98-99). At first, the world of appearance and experience seems to guarantee a future that is still dark and unknown.

The new riddle that now confronts Oedipus is the discovery of the source of the plague in the underlying pollution which is its cause. With Apollo's response, the hunt for Laios' murderer and the source of this pollution begins, and the language of the play comes to be controlled by the metaphors of the hunt: discovery, paths and wandering, inference, conjecture, and revelation. What is dark will be brought to light. The murder of Laios is ancient history, but Oedipus' wit searches for the one clue that could teach him the rest (145). What he is looking for are signs or tokens (*semeia, symbola*). These are at the heart of Oedipus' quest (295). A *symbolon* (or *semeion*) is the half of a whole that has been broken—a joint or a tally.[1] Oedipus attempts to fit pieces together to gain a picture of the whole, and he is looking for the tallies that brought together strangers and the members of broken families. It is characteristic of Oedipus' intelligence that it makes of the world of appearance the half that will fit into a larger whole. He believes that the obscure and unknown can be seen in the face of appearances.

It is Oedipus' confidence that the invisible can be read in the physiognomy of the visible that controls his language and actions. In his flight from Corinth and the man and woman he considered his father and mother, Oedipus takes his bearings on the distant and invisible when he measures his distance from Corinth by the stars (1035). When the shepherd who saved him from death on Mt.

---

1. For the range and sense of the word *symbolon*, consider the word as it describes the two sexes as broken halves of a primordial whole in Plato, *Symposium* 191 D, and compare Empedocles, *Fragment* B 63. *Semeia*, the tokens that led to the recognition of blood-ties in Greek tragedy, are discussed by Aristotle in the *Poetics*, Chapter 16; cf., in their contexts, Euripides *Electra* 577; *Ion* 1386; and in comedy, Menander, *The Arbitration* (*Epitrepontes* 331-333), and *Rape of the Locks* (*Perikeiromene* 135).

Kithairon appears as Oedipus' last hope and the last piece in the puzzle of his life (cf. 1334), Oedipus does not recognize him. But he can guess who he must be. There is a harmony and measure between the unknown shepherd and the man he sees before him (1408-1409). When the Corinthian arrives to announce the death of Polybos, Oedipus asks him to "convey" or "signify" to him news of his father's death. "Convey" rather than "tell" because Oedipus has no immediate knowledge of Polybos' death or what is happening in Corinth. And when he has heard the Messenger's oblique account, he attempts to make the news of Polybos' death join with the oracle that he was fated to kill his father. If he died "from wanting me to be with him," then you could say that I killed him.

The very actions and conjectures which distract Oedipus in his search for the truth speak eloquently for his character. He is intelligent, quick to act and react, political, suspicious. He is quick to spot a plot in the murder of Laios, for he is not satisfied that the man who was king before him could have been killed by bandits acting alone. They must be part of a plot hatched in Thebes (148-150). Oedipus is also a man who sees himself as acting and reacting alone at the center of things. Kreon and the one survivor of the attack on Laios both speak of "bandits," but Oedipus strangely speaks of the bandit. His language is surely governed by the plot of Sophocles' play, but it must be determined too by Oedipus' sense of himself as an individual at the center of his actions—one man in control of things, and not part of a group. He is affected by the plague as no one else. He places himself at the heart of his city's sufferings, for he suffers for his city, for himself, and for the priest and the others he sees before him (85).

The question he asks of Delphi is what can I do or say to save my city (93). Apollo's response requires action: drive out the man who is polluting Thebes with the stain of Laios' blood upon him. What makes Oedipus impervious to Teiresias' accusation that he, Oedipus, is the killer of Laios, and worse, is his interpretation of these words as the face of a plot Kreon has constructed against him. Oedipus' political instinct and his sense of himself are so strong that he can tell Jocasta that Kreon is plotting against his "person" and shift the curse he had laid on the murderer of Laios onto Kreon (842-844). Voltaire complained in his *Lettre III* on Sophocles' *Oedipus* (1719) that Oedipus absurdly went about consulting oracles and pronouncing curses rather than discovering the one witness to the murderer of Laios. It seemed implausible (*invraisemblable*) that a king who wanted to get to the bottom of things would act as Oedipus does.[2] But in truth, Oedipus' estimate of human nature is plausible. What is absurd in Sophocles' *Oedipus* is the fact that the events of Oedipus' own life were not subject to the control of human intelligence. At the end, Kreon says as much.

Oedipus first appears strikingly both as what he is and seems. He tells the world that he is Oedipus—"Everybody everywhere knows who I am: Oedipus. King." Oedipus is already known to the group of Thebans who sit at the altars of his palace. And he is known to Sophocles' audience.[3] Behind Oedipus' words, which seem so incongruous to a modern sense of realism, is a requirement of full disclosure. What is known must be brought out into the open for all to see. Kreon is obliged to tell Oedipus and Sophocles' audience (127-128):

My lord, before you came to Thebes, before you came to power,
Laios was our king.

Oedipus must tell Jocasta, his wife of many years: "My father was Polybos, of Corinth. My mother Merope, was Dorian." The requirement for illumination of the obvious, the imperious need to bring the background into the foreground, might seem Homeric. What Oedipus tells his wife about his family is as incongruous to a standard of realism as it is true to a demand for full disclosure. In the *Iliad*, Homer responds to this demand when he has Helen identify to Priam the Greeks who have been waging war against him for ten years (3.162-242). Homer and his audience want to contemplate the world, no matter how familiar it might seem, set out clearly before them. But in Sophocles the statement of the obvious has still another motive. What is obvious is brought out into the open to reveal the dark background and shadowy past the audience could see behind the stage building of the palace and the apparent sense of the words of the actors. This background is revealed in Oedipus' response to Kreon's description of Laios: "I know. But I never saw Laios." Oedipus had seen Laios, once, at or near a place where three roads meet.

2. *Oeuvres Complètes de Voltaire: 2 Théatre I* (1877) *Lettre III* (on Sophocles' *Oedipus*), pp. 18-28. Voltaire's long list of Sophocles' violations of the "rules of common sense" shows an unparalleled acuteness to the surface contradictions and "unrealistic" details of the plot of the *Oedipus* and a resolute and confident obtuseness to the genius of Sophoclean irony.

3. Before the presentation of his play itself, Sophocles had mounted a platform and announced to his audience the title of his play and its theme—a practice discussed by Pickard-Cambridge, *The Dramatic Festivals of Athens*[2] (Oxford 1968) 67-68.

A part of this background are the memories that gradually come to threaten Oedipus and his sense of control and security. At first, he seems secure and nearly a god. The Thebans who have come to his palace gather before *his* altars. He is master of Thebes (52). Yet even his first words, when they have become a matter for reflection, betray an insecurity. He calls the group of suppliants "children" and so associates himself with his people and their history. Oedipus seems stable, the pilot of the ship of state, but he is a man without roots. He has come to Thebes and Jocasta as a harbor (582, 1548). He looks for security and roots in Thebes, in kingship and marriage to the wife of the murdered king. His search for the murderer is something he does for Laios "as for my own murdered father" and "for every royal generation of Thebes" (361-366). His thought of all that binds him to Laios—the kingship of Thebes, the same bed and the same wife, and even the possibility of common children by this wife—speaks for the same thing. His doubts and uneasiness about his origin seem to spring from an episode in Corinth when a drunken companion told him that he was not his father's son. The word that injured Oedipus was *plastos* —bastard, a fabrication (1023). What Oedipus wants to discover is not art or artifice but nature: his origins, his seed, his nature, the truth. He is not sure that he knows the truth about himself. Apollo would not give him an answer when he went from Corinth to Delphi to discover the truth about his origins (1025). None of Teiresias' prophecies strike home to Oedipus, but one word touches him (597-601):

TEIRESIAS Call me fool, if you like, but your parents,
        who gave you life, they respected my judgment.
OEDIPUS Parents?
                What do you mean?
                            Who are my mother and father?

Oedipus' doubts about his origins break out in this startled reaction.

There is another moment like this in the play. It comes when Jocasta confidently tries to show Oedipus how little trust can be placed in oracles. She will bring to light (*phanō*) decisive indications (*semeia*) of what she says. There was an oracle that Laios would be killed by his son, but robbers killed him—at the three ways. These words stun Oedipus. His memory of what happened near the three ways moves him to wander over old and new paths of fear and memory (953; cf. 90). He is so lost in thought that he does not register what Jocasta goes on to tell him about how her son died, with his ankles pierced and strung together, on a mountain where there are no roads or people. One join in the puzzle of his life prevents him from making another that could connect his old wound and his name (Oedipus, Swollenfoot) with Jocasta's son. For Oedipus, the phrase "at the three ways" is the first path he encounters, and this is the path he takes.

When Oedipus takes over the search for the murderer of Laios, he speaks as a god and prophet:

I will begin the search again, I
will reveal the truth, expose everything

He will bring the truth to light (phanō, 162). Both Oedipus and Jocasta use the language of prophecy, and unwittingly they become prophets. Jocasta's revelation comes at the turning point of the play, for with her proofs the action turns from the public to the private, from the search for the murderer of Laios to Oedipus and his past which is haunted by oracles. Just as it seems that the oracles concerning Laios have lost their life, and the Chorus are shaken in their confidence in the gods, the Messenger from Corinth arrives. Jocasta's prayer to Apollo to "help us purify ourselves of this disease" (1170) is answered. Moments before the Chorus had put a condition on their worship of the gods (1144-1151):

no
I will never go to the holy untouchable stone
navel of the earth at Delphi
never again
go to the temples at Olympia at Abai
if all these things are not joined
if past present future are not made one
made clear to mortal eyes

They will no longer dance. But in their dance to honor the god Dionysos, all the pieces of the oracles of the gods fit together. Symbola join. And Oedipus, whose intelligence and passion have driven him to seek his origins and to seek in the world around him equalities and commensurability, succeeds in bringing to light his life "from its very beginning." He has discovered his nature (physis).

At the end of the play, all of the pieces of the puzzle of Oedipus' life fit together, beautifully, into a tale of sound and fury, told by a dramatic artist of supreme genius. In Sophocles' Oedipus art and nature come together. But they are incommensurable. Sophocles' art can reveal the darkness of Oedipus' life and origins. It cannot imitate it or explain it. The artistry of the Oedipus bespeaks a world of purpose and design. The underlying tale of Oedipus' life has no purpose or design. The servant who tells what went on within the palace speaks of "wailing, madness, shame and death, every evil men have given a name" (1657-1658). The tale of Oedipus' life makes no sense. Of all the questions asked in the Oedipus, one is not asked: Why did Oedipus suffer what he suffered.

II

Apollo and Zeus comprehend. They know and understand how human affairs stand. As for mortal men, no human can be called a better prophet than another (675-684). In their response to the accusations and prophecies of Teiresias, the Chorus establish a boundary between gods and men. The gods "grasp everything." The word means that they can put things together. They are xunetoí, they comprehend (cf. 1149-1150). In the Oedipus, only two mortals know how the pieces of Oedipus' life fit together: Teiresias and the old shepherd who saved Oedipus' life. The Chorus say of Teiresias that he is the only man in whom truth is inborn (411). Oedipus says of him that he knows what can be taught and what must be locked in silence: the things of the heavens and the things that move upon the earth (413-414). The very syntax of this sentence crosses the human and the divine. On the higher level are things that must be locked in silence (arrheta) and the things of the heavens. On the lower level are the things that can be taught and the things that move upon the earth. Teiresias' knowledge comprehends heaven and earth. Despite his reluctance, he is compelled to say the unspeakable. In the Oedipus heaven and earth come together. What is revealed about the life of one man is unspeakable.

At the beginning of the play the gods appear as closer to men than they do at the end. The smoke and prayers rising up from plague-stricken Thebes appear to join gods and men. The city and its king look to the gods for the beginning and end of their grief. It is the priest of Zeus who speaks for Thebes. And when Kreon returns from Delphi, his face is bright and flushed, and still seems to reflect the brilliance of the place (100-101). He is wearing a garland of laurel, heavy with berry clusters. In their entrance song the Chorus sing of Delphi where the voice of the god is music (aduepes). They call Thebes "bright." Their song puts a beautiful and radiant face on all of the gods but Ares and Hades. It is full of light. Hope is the bright seed of the future. Apollo's bowstring is twisted with gold thread. The daughter of Zeus is golden. The Chorus ask her to send them the "warm bright face of peace of help of our salvation" Artemis dances on the mountains "sowing light where your feet brush the ground" The faces of the gods are bright; Dionysos' "blazing like the sea when the sun falls on it." The Chorus ask him to roar with the face of fire on the murderer of Laios, and they call upon Zeus to destroy the fire of plague with the fire of his lightning.

At the beginning of the Oedipus, the things of heaven are bright, immortal, radiant. They seem near to Thebes. But as the divine help the city prays for draws nearer, Parnassos, Olympos, and the "huge clear fields of heaven" of the second stasimon retreat into the distance. The gods are referred to less and less frequently. Yet the brilliance of the entrance song of the Chorus is not a façade disguising the darkness of the world Oedipus penetrates at the end of the play. It casts its light on what happens in the play. It is the language that first describes Ares, the god the gods would drive from heaven (apotimon, 283), that comes to describe Oedipus. And the striking image of the murderer of Laios as a lonely bull, wandering "among caves and grey rocks cut from the herd" (655-657), comes to describe Oedipus who will be driven from Thebes.

In the bloody, mutilated face of Oedipus, the Chorus can see the warm, bright face of the peace they had prayed for (243). But it is not Apollo with a wall of arrows, or Zeus with his lightning, or Dionysos with his blazing pine torch, that destroys "Ares" and the source of the plague. It is Oedipus who sinks the brooches he tore from the body of his wife and mother into eyes that have seen and failed to see too much. These brooches were of beaten gold (1634). This is the last reference to gold in the play. In Oedipus' face we seem to see for a moment the face of things human and the last and faint reflection of things divine.

A modern audience asks why Oedipus blinded himself. But this is not the question the Chorus asks (1728-1738):

CHORUS What you did was horrible,
    but how could you quench the fire of your eyes,
    what demon lifted your hands?

OEDIPUS Apollo Apollo
    it was Apollo, always Apollo,
    who brought each of my agonies to birth,
    but I,
    nobody else, I,

> I raised these two hands of mine, held them above my head,
> and plunged them down,
> I stabbed out these eyes.

The question the Chorus ask springs from a common belief, and a common need to find the sources of human action outside the self. For the Chorus, the demonic is the explanation for the violent, inexplicable, more than human shifts in men's actions. Some *outside* force, some god or devil, must have stirred Oedipus to do what he did. But if "Apollo" were Oedipus' full answer to the question of the Chorus, he would lose his last illusion of responsibility for his actions. Oedipus reveals his character in its deepest places when he says "I, I raised these two hands . . . I stabbed out these eyes." A man's inner character is his *daimon*.[4] In his unalienable conviction that he can control his life, Oedipus stands apart from and above those who surround him. The Chorus attribute Oedipus' success with the Sphinx to some god who gave him what he needed to free Thebes (58). Oedipus attributes it to himself (536). When Oedipus is at the point of discovering the answer to the riddle of his own life, his agitation frightens Jocasta so much that she comes out to the altar of Apollo to pray for some solution. Despite her proclaimed scepticism about oracles, she believes that Oedipus' strange behavior, his agitation and his passion to know the truth, must be brought on by some god. So she prays to Apollo who is "close to my life" (1168). This too is the belief of the household servant who witnessed Oedipus' rage and self-mutilation. Oedipus was taken over by "some god, some demon" (1619). Some devil showed him the way to his wife. In the last choral song, human happiness (*eudaimonia*) is just that—"hap"—luck with the hidden and incomprehensible powers of the gods. Oedipus had none of this luck. He and his destiny are *dysdaimon*. His very life, which is the perfect expression of the dark abyss beneath human life, is a *daimon* (1518-1519). Some demon leapt on him (1684), as bad luck had leapt on his father (359), and cleared the gap between appearance and reality.

But in the tale of Oedipus' life, of his *daimon*, there is one action that did not come from the outside and that was not a passion, but

---

4. This is Heraclitus' reply to the Homeric and common Greek conception of a *daimon* external to a man's character as controlling and explaining the strange and exceptional in his actions and behaviour. In Homer, the clearest expression of this notion is the word *daimonie*. When Paris is strangely moved to stay in bed with Helen rather than fighting the Greeks on the plain of Troy, Hector tries to call him to his senses: *daimonie* (*Iliad* 6.521; cf. 326)—which is best translated "What's got into you?". Heraclitus' response to this mode of thought is "a man's character is his 'daimon,'" Fragment B 119 (Diels-Kranz).

something he willed and did knowingly. He put out his eyes. Except for this, the action of the *Oedipus* could be called a "passion." The Chorus do not get an answer they could be content with. Oedipus' life belonged to Apollo, but his blindness he claims for himself. When he has seen what was hidden behind the visible façade of his life, he can no longer look upon the new reality that has come to the surface. Without moving an inch, Oedipus fulfills his curse and drives himself from Thebes and the bright, shining statues of the gods (*agalmata*, 1792). Or rather he banishes them, since for the Chorus and the audience in the theater of Dionysos, it is Oedipus who remains at the center of things.

The outline of his life was drawn by Apollo. Oedipus' only free action is to blot out this outline. For him, the visible does not wear the face of things unseen. The sight (*opsis*) of his parents is no longer "the sweetest thing on earth" (1780-1782). Blind, he can put from him, or attempt to, the unspeakable things of the heavens. He has seen enough of what can be told by men—of the things that "move upon the ground." The significance of his action can be stated simply, in terms that are Greek and taken from a language in which knowledge is the memory of things seen: *Oida*, "I have seen," "I know," is a part of Oedipus' name:

By nature all men have a craving for knowledge. One sign of this is the love they have for their senses, for apart from their usefulness they are loved for themselves, and more than any other, the sense of sight. For men prefer sight to practically anything else, not only as a means to doing something but even when they intend to do nothing at all. The reason for this love is that more than the other senses, sight makes it possible to discern reality and reveals many distinctions. (Aristotle, *Metaphysics* A 1.980a; translated by Diskin Clay)

III

The world of the actors in Greek tragedy does not have the same integrity as that of the audience seated in the theater of Dionysos. The audience have a godlike vantage on the action of the play. They comprehend in its outline the story of Oedipus' life. But their knowledge of what is fated to happen to Oedipus is not exactly that of the gods, for what the human spectators know is the past, and this knowledge is expressed in their myths. The gods know past, present, and future. Their knowledge is expressed not in myth, but in prophecy. Their oracles are alive (660). In time, their prophecies "come out," like Apollo and like the sun (1274-1277, 1492). If the vantage of the gods and Sophocles' audience is similar in that they both contemplate the fate of a man who does not know his fate, men and gods react differently to what they see. The gods of the *Oedipus* are not the gods of the *Iliad* and *Odyssey* who occasionally, in the case of some men at least, are moved to look down on human sufferings and human fate with interest, compassion, and involvement. In Sophocles' *Oedipus*, the "gazing gods" do not "lean forward from the sky" (Pope's brilliant rendition of *Iliad* 22.218). Only men feel pity. It is the pity felt by a slave that made the horrors of Oedipus' life possible (1486), and these horrors inspire pity (1576-1577). But the gods remain distant, radiant, and clear. They are constantly called upon by humans. But as their workings become more visible in the play, the gods themselves seem to grow more remote. After Jocasta has caught sight of the truth and rushed into the palace, the Chorus sing of the gods for the last time. They ask if their king, who thinks that he is the son of Luck, is not part divine—the son of some god who walks the mountains: of Pan and a mountain nymph, or Apollo, or Hermes. The last words of their song conjure up a vision of Dionysos at play with the nymphs of Helicon (1404). A final illusion drifts cloud-like, brightly, insubstantially over the darkness of the truth. And when the Chorus give articulation to their thought and feeling for the last time in the play, the gods have nearly disappeared. They can only speak of Oedipus' life as a *daimon* and cry out "o Zeus" (1527). Oedipus is *atheos*—godless (1774). But the only emotion attributed to the gods of the *Oedipus* is anger and their hatred for Oedipus (1967). There is nothing in Sophocles' treatment of his life and family that could explain that hatred.

The dramatic irony of Sophocles' *Oedipus* is not an isolated, surface phenomenon. It comes from the gap that opens up between gods and men, appearance and reality. In the agony of his discoveries, Oedipus finds the perfect expression for this gap: "how beautiful I was when you sheltered me as a child and oh what disease festered beneath that beauty" (1812-1813). There are moments when this disease breaks through the surface of the play; when the illusory world of the drama on stage is disrupted by the demonic forces at work in Sophocles' plot. Early on, Oedipus says that he will do all he can to find the murderer of Laios "as I would fight for my own murdered father" (361). Sophocles' audience is in the divine position of knowing the truth and knowing that Oedipus is blind to the truth of what he says. But Sophoclean irony is more complex than this textbook example.

The language of the play is under the control of a force larger than its human actors. This is the demonic force of the plot. Kreon speaks of the bandits who killed Laios; but Oedipus speaks of the bandit (148). He asks Kreon "Who is the man? Who is Apollo's victim?" (126), and is uneasy that the same man who killed Laios might want to take his revenge on Oedipus with the same violent hand (169). Revenge. Oedipus' choice of this strange word is explained only at the end of the play when he takes his revenge on the murderer with the same violent hand that killed Laios. The killer is called the man whose hand did the deed (autocheir, 367). When he has blinded himself, Oedipus stands before the Chorus and says: "I raised these two hands of mine (autocheir) . . . I stabbed out these eyes."

Teiresias knows the unspeakable. His inner vision opens up to him past, present, and future. He was not on stage to hear the curse Oedipus lays on the murderer of Laios (339-341). But when he repeats this curse in the prophecy of the grim future he sees for Oedipus (591), some demonic presence is felt on stage. This same presence makes itself felt as the memory of Oedipus' past begins to come to the surface of the play. In her futile attempt to reassure Oedipus, Jocasta speaks of the place where Laios was killed by robbers as at the meeting of three ways. But Oedipus' memory is more precise. Laios was not murdered. He was cut down—near a crossroads (cf. 956 and 1040).

The gods' vision of the future and the audience's knowledge of the outlines of Oedipus' past are concentrated on the stage of the theater of Dionysos. Prophecy and myth have the same point of focus. Jocasta speaks of the voices of prophecy which "gave shape" (diorisan) to a future in which Laios would be killed by his son (948). Oedipus speaks of the same thing when he looks back on his past. He thinks of himself as the son of a benevolent Luck (tyche, 1368-1373).

I am like the months, my brothers the months—they shaped me
when I was a baby in the cold hills of Kithairon,
they guided me, carved out my times of greatness,
and they still move their hands over my life.

The months "shaped" Oedipus (diorisan, 1370). But when he finally sees the shape of his life, he blots it out.

When Oedipus is led out from his palace to face, without seeing, the Chorus and Thebes, Sophocles seems to be asking a question of his audience. It can be put in the form of a riddle: "There is a creature which moves upon the earth on two feet, on four, and on three. He has one name." At the end of the Oedipus, this riddle seems not so much a question as a prophecy. And indeed in their last song the Chorus call the Sphinx the singer of a "song of the future" (1530). The song of the Sphinx is still another version of the story of Oedipus. As the play opens, Oedipus stands upright and securely, at the height of his power. He has helped Thebes stand up straight again. But he began life as a maimed and helpless infant on Kithairon. He could barely crawl. At the end of his life he will need a staff to feel his way to another country. The answer to the riddle of the Sphinx is man, but Oedipus is not Everyman. He has suffered and done too much. The power of his life and the darkness he has penetrated as he sees the light bring him to the country of Teiresias' prophecy, to Athens and the awful groves of the Furies. It is this power (menos) that is felt and commemorated in Sophocles' last play, which he set in his own deme of Kolonos.

When they left the theater of Dionysos, Sophocles' godlike Athenians returned to the life of their city and the plague that was ravaging Athens. Outside the theater of Dionysos, they lost their divinity and had to face the demonic forces that break into human life and disrupt human calculation (cf. the daimonia of Thucydides II 64). This is the ultimate Sophoclean irony.

IV

Oedipus is the source of the plague that wastes Thebes. He is the end of the inquest into the murder of Laios. But the revulsion of nature expressed in the plague, and the reaction of the Chorus to "crimes unnameable things" (636), seem out of proportion to what first appears to be the crime of a stranger or strangers in a foreign country. It is only in the speech of the palace servant at the end of the play that words are found for the unspeakable. Raging within the palace Oedipus proclaims what he is. He wants to reveal to Thebes the man who murdered his father, the man—but the servant cannot bring himself to repeat what Oedipus said of his mother (1666). It is unspeakable. The horror and fascination of the unspeakable are at the heart of the final scene of the Oedipus. When Oedipus emerges from his palace he is blind; his mask is bloodstained. He has the stain of his father's blood upon him. He has committed incest. His children are his brothers and sisters. He stands in the light of the sun, and the very elements recoil before him. He is no longer king of Thebes. He is no longer a man. He is a thing—"this cursed, naked, holy thing, hide him from the earth and the sacred rain and the light" (1852-1853). Oedipus has become an *agos*, something both sacred and cursed, and by the end of the play his curse has extended in its range from Thebes to the natural world.

The unspeakable holds much of the wisdom of the dramatic festivals which Athens held to honor the god Dionysos. The Athenians who came to witness the dramatic contests witnessed and heard named the most terrible things that could occur in the work-a-day life of their *polis*. During the rest of the year the words for the things represented on stage were dangerous. Except perhaps in Greece, there is no way of conveying to a modern audience, who live a world apart from the intense, close, public, curious, jealous, and family-centered world of Athens, the horror and fascination of the words for those who beat or killed their fathers or mothers, or the citizen soldier who abandoned his shield in battle. *Patrophonos*—father killer. These words were sticks and stones. They stirred up feelings that came from a deep sense of family and of civic identity. The repressed feelings created by tight family and civic bonds were expressed in the festivals of Dionysos. On the tragic stage the Athenian spectator could see parents who kill and devour their children; children who strike and murder their parents; wives who kill their husbands. And on this stage incest, a thing for which there is no proper name in Greek, was spoken of. But in their everyday lives, and in the Athenian courts of law, men spoke of "the kind of marriages that happen in tragedies."

The dramatic festivals were a time of freedom that made life in Athens livable. In the fourth century, prisoners were released from jail and no debts could be contracted. It was a time of freedom of speech (*parrhesia*) when Athenians could hear, if not repeat, words of terrible fascination. This begins to reveal the significance of Aristotle's observations that the plots of Greek tragedy were taken mainly from the stories of great families and that the kind of learning peculiar to tragedy was the recognition of blood ties.[5]

In the larger context of the social function of Greek tragedy, Oedipus can be seen as an everyman—the sleeping man in every city who cannot live in political society. This everyman resembles the tyrant who makes his brief appearance at the very center of the *Oedipus*. The great antistrophe beginning (1115)

arrogance insatiable pride
breed the tyrant

is a part of the Chorus' reaction to the implications of Jocasta's words of comfort to Oedipus. A disbelief in the oracles of the gods, however

5. *Poetics* 13.1453a19, and 9.1452a31.

qualified and hedged, threatens to destroy the fabric of the city and raise in its place the grim and ancient figure of the *tyrannos*. One commentary to the reflections of the Chorus on piety, arrogance, and tyranny comes from Socrates' description of the *tyrannos* who sleeps in the soul of waking men. When the higher parts of the soul sleep, it wakes:

The beastly and wild part, gorged with food or drink, is skittish and, pushing sleep away, seeks to satisfy its dispositions . . . in such a state it dares to do everything as though it were released from, and rid of, all shame and prudence. And it doesn't shrink from attempting intercourse, as it supposes, with a mother . . . or attempting any foul murder at all. (*Republic* IX 571 c, trans. Allan Bloom)

The Chorus seem to take Oedipus into the net of their allusion. The words of caution they offered Oedipus are words for a man careful not to *stumble* (807), and Oedipus has told Thebes that with god's help he and his city will be revealed as lucky or *fallen* (cf. 178). The words of the Chorus now seem to hit home. They call up a familiar vision of the tyrant's climb and plunge from a place where he can't put his feet anywhere (1120-1123). *Feet*. The word hobbles behind Oedipus throughout the play (cf. 642). *Breeds*, too, seems to reflect Oedipus' attempt to know himself by discovering who his parents were.

But just as the net of allusion seems to tighten about the king of Thebes, Oedipus slips out (1125-1127):

but let men compete let self-perfection grow
let men sharpen their skills
soldiers citizens building the good city

This struggle is Oedipus' struggle. The movement of the antistrophe of this *stasimon* repeats the movement of the last antistrophe of the first *stasimon*. Then the Chorus free Oedipus from the heavy and obscure charges Teiresias brings against him by reflecting back on his struggle for Thebes (685-690). If the *tyrannos* the Chorus call up comes from "the cursed thoughts that Nature gives way to in repose" (*Macbeth* II i 8), he also comes from another age. He haunts Sophocles' stage for a moment, touching untouchable things, fed on thing after thing, endlessly, giving no reverence to the shrines of the gods. He has a major but mute part to play in Sophocles' *Oedipus*. At the end of the play there is no talk of Oedipus' *fall*. Rather the Chorus speak of the storm of disaster that has overwhelmed him (1983), and the god or devil that leapt on him (1684).

The moment the Chorus finish their song about the tyrant who "does not fear justice fear the gods bow to their shining presences," Jocasta appears before the altar of Apollo with offerings. The role of the *tyrannos* of the second *stasimon* is like that of the family quarrel (*neikos*) of the first. In looking to the past, to a family cursed by a quarrel and, for a moment, to the figure the *tyrannos*, Sophocles is opening and closing the doors of his stage to one explanation of the story of Oedipus. In Sophocles, the fate of Oedipus does not have the familiar and intelligible shape of the fate of a *tyrannos* or a character caught up in a family curse. His Oedipus is not an Agamemnon, caught up in the second generation of an inherited curse and acting like a *tyrannos*, or an Eteokles, whose fate was sealed by the acts of his grandfather and the curses of his father.[6]

At the end of his discoveries, Oedipus is the object of horrible curiosity. Kreon calls him "this cursed, naked, holy thing" (1852). He is an *agos*—both cursed and sacred. And all of Kreon's safe and prudent maxims do not support him in the moment of his terrible isolation. All things are not good in their proper time (1962). Natures such as his are hardest to bear (894), and the heavy burden he has to bear, once it has been made clear, brings him neither luck nor peace (105-106). One day has shown Oedipus to be as "evil" and as unhappy in his parents as a man can be (803). The earlier and haunting images of the god the gods would drive from them and the solitary bull who has been cut from its herd (657) have come to gather around the solitary figure of Oedipus. This object of universal revulsion is still a man. He has banished from him the world in which the unknown joined beautifully with what he thought he knew. It made no sense. He still calls upon the gods, but he can no longer see their bright stone statues. Yet he still wants to be the master of his own life. His one free act was to put out his eyes. And his last act is to reach out to his daughters, to the things that remain dearest to him, and clasp them to him.

V

What Oedipus discovers is the story repeated in handbooks of Greek mythology. It goes something like this:

Laios and Jocasta are told by an oracle that Laios will be killed by a son. Jocasta has a son. She gives him to a shepherd to expose on Mt. Kithairon,

6. Within the space I have, I develop my reasons for this interpretation of Sophocle's treatment of the Oedipus myth in the notes to 196, 669, and 1115.

but the shepherd pities the baby and gives him to another shepherd, who gives him to Polybos, king of Corinth. Polybos and his wife Merope bring him up as their son. One day a drunken companion tells Oedipus that he is not his father's son. Oedipus goes to Delphi to learn the truth of these words, but can learn nothing except that he is fated to kill his father, marry his mother, and have children by her. To frustrate this prophecy he decides to keep away from Corinth, and on his way down from Delphi he meets Laios, who is on his way there to consult the oracle, is provoked, kills Laios and all of his companions but one. He then goes to Thebes and frees the town from the Sphinx by solving her riddle, marries the widowed queen, has four children by her. A plague breaks out in Thebes, and in his search for the cause of the plague, Oedipus discovers the story of his life and blinds himself.

In the *Iliad* we hear of the funeral of the "fallen" Oedipus (23.679), but learn nothing about how he fell. In the *Odyssey*, Odysseus catches sight of Epikaste in Hades and tells the Phaeacians a part of her story (11.271-280). In her ignorance she did a "great deed" and married her son who had killed his father. Odysseus says that the gods made this known, but he does not say how. Oedipus continues to be king of Thebes "through the baneful designs of the gods," but Epikaste hangs herself and leaves her son the Furies that avenge a dead mother.

We have no ancient date for the *Oedipus*, but Bernard Knox must be right in seeing in the association of Ares with the plague in Thebes a reflection of the plague that erupted in Athens in the second year of the Peloponnesian war and flared up again in 425. On the internal evidence of the play, taken with Thucydides' description of the plague, 425 is as close as we can come to a date for its first production.[7] Oedipus' name means Swollenfoot but it can also be translated Witfoot—the man who knows or is known by his foot. The conventional title of the play is *Oedipus Tyrannos*, or *Oedipus the King*. But the original title was probably *Oedipus*, and *tyrannos* later served to distinguish it from the *Oedipus at Kolonos*. We have yielded to tradition and given it the title *Oedipus the King*.

VI

The text of this translation is the Greek text printed by Jebb, *Sophocles: I The Oedipus Tyrannus*, Cambridge 1887.[2] Our translation attempts a solution to the problems of the text at 622-627, which Jebb

7. "The Date of the Oedipus Tyrannus," *American Journal of Philology* 77 (1956), 133-47.

attempted to solve by a necessary transposition of lines and an unnecessary lacuna (see the note to 815-816). We have been helped by his commentary to the play and that of J. C. Kamerbeek, *The Plays of Sophocles: IV The Oedipus Tyrannus*, Leiden 1967. An even more valuable commentary was Bernard Knox's *Oedipus at Thebes*, New Haven 1957. I learned much about the play from J. B. McDiarmid when I studied it with him in the fall of 1961. Joseph Russo has read my Introduction, and I thank him for being Oedipus to some of the oracles I pronounced in an earlier version.

Baltimore, Maryland   DISKIN CLAY
March 1977

A NOTE ON THE CHORUSES

I have not punctuated the choruses because they fluctuate somewhere between talk and song and lack many of the usual bridges of logic found in prose syntax. Also, I wanted to distinguish them from the rest of the play, musically, since they are a consciousness separate from the action and thought of the characters, though deeply involved with events as they occur. Perhaps terms like "broken song" or "chant"—speech free to range from the conversational to the lyrical through exclamation, narration, exposition, description—are definitions which help us to grasp the structural attitude of the choruses. Without Greek, I had to imagine something in English bred by the original as I found it described by Diskin Clay, Jebb, and other experts, something which today's reader and audience would find both strange, immediate, and convincing, something fifteen people could say as if they were one. I can think of no corresponding voice in our society, no single expression of authority which, when we hear it, we feel we must believe. I shaped the choruses to catch that power, and to establish the fluidity of contact with and response to each action, each wave of consciousness which the choral voice must reflect.

Philadelphia, Pennsylvania   STEPHEN BERG
July 1977

OEDIPUS THE KING

CHARACTERS

OEDIPUS   king of Thebes

PRIEST   of Zeus

KREON   Oedipus' brother-in-law

CHORUS   of Theban elders

LEADER   of the chorus

TEIRESIAS   prophet, servant to Apollo

JOCASTA   wife of Oedipus

MESSENGER   from Corinth

SHEPHERD   member of Laios' household

SERVANT   household slave of Oedipus

Delegation of Thebans, servants to lead Teiresias and Oedipus; attendants to Oedipus, Kreon, Jocasta; and Antigone and Ismene, the daughters of Oedipus.

Line numbers in the right-hand margin of the text refer to the English translation only, and the Notes at p. 101 are keyed to these lines. The bracketed line numbers in the running headlines refer to the Greek text.

Dawn. Silence. The royal palace of Thebes. The altar of Apollo to the left of the central palace. A delegation of Thebans—old men, boys, young children—enters the orchestra by the steps below the altar, assembles, and waits. They carry suppliant boughs—olive branches tied with strips of wool. Some climb the steps between the orchestra and the altar, place their branches on the altar, and return to the orchestra. A PRIEST stands apart from the suppliants at the foot of one of the two stairs. Silence. Waiting. The central doors open. From inside the palace, limping, OEDIPUS comes through the palace doors and stands at the top of the steps leading down into the orchestra. He is dressed in gold and wears a golden crown.

OEDIPUS Why, children,
        why are you here, why
        are you holding those branches tied with wool,
        begging me for help? Children,
        the whole city smolders with incense.
        Wherever I go I hear sobbing, praying. Groans fill the air.
        Rumors, news from messengers, they are not enough for me.
        Others cannot tell me what you need.
        I am king, I had to come. As king,
        I had to know. Know for myself, know for me.   10
        Everybody everywhere knows who I am: Oedipus. King.
        Priest of Zeus, we respect your age, your high office.
        Speak.
        Why are you kneeling? Are you afraid, old man?
        What can I give you?
        How can I help? Ask.
        Ask me anything. Anything at all.
        My heart would be a stone
        if I felt no pity for these poor shattered people of mine
        kneeling here, at my feet.   20

PRIEST Oedipus, lord of Thebes, you see us, the people of Thebes, your people,

crowding in prayer around your altar,

these small children here, old men bent with age, priests, and I, the priest of Zeus,

and our noblest young men, the pride and strength of Thebes.

And there are more of us, lord Oedipus, more—gathered in the city, stunned,

kneeling, offering their branches, praying before the two great temples of Athena

or staring into the ashes of burnt offerings, staring,

waiting, waiting for the god to speak.

Look,

look at it,   30

lord Oedipus—right there,

in front of your eyes—this city—

it reels under a wild storm of blood, wave after wave battering Thebes.

We cannot breathe or stand.

We hunger, our world shivers with hunger. A disease hungers,

nothing grows, wheat, fruit, nothing grows bigger than a seed.

Our women bear

dead things,

all they can do is grieve,

our cattle wither, stumble, drop to the ground,   40

flies simmer on their bloated tongues,

the plague spreads everywhere, a stain seeping through our streets, our fields, our houses,

look—god's fire eating everyone, everything,

stroke after stroke of lightning, the god stabbing it alive—

it can't be put out, it can't be stopped,

its heat thickens the air, it glows like smoking metal,

this god of plague guts our city and fills the black world under us where the dead go

with the shrieks of women,

living women, wailing.

You are a man, not a god—I know.   50

We all know this, the young kneeling here before you know
    it, too,

but we know how great you are, Oedipus, greater than any
    man.

When crisis struck, you saved us here in Thebes,

you faced the mysterious, strange disasters hammered against
    us by the gods.

This is our history—

we paid our own flesh to the Sphinx until you set us free.

You knew no more than anyone, but you knew.

There was a god in it, a god in you.

The PRIEST kneels.

Help us. Oedipus, we beg you, we all turn to you, kneeling
    to your greatness.

Advice from the gods or advice from human beings—you   60
    will know which is needed.

But help us. Power and experience are yours, all yours.

Between thought and action, between

our plans and their results a distance opens.

Only a man like you, Oedipus, tested by experience,

can make them one. That much I know.

Oedipus, more like a god than any man alive,

deliver us, raise us to our feet. Remember who you are.

Remember your love for Thebes. Your skill was our salvation
    once before.

For this Thebes calls you savior.

Don't let us remember you as the king—godlike in power—   70

who gave us back our life, then let us die.

Steady us forever. You broke the riddle for us then.

It was a sign. A god was in it. Be the man you were—

rule now as you ruled before.

Oh Oedipus,

how much better to rule a city of men than be king of
    empty earth.

A city is nothing, a ship is nothing

where no men live together, where no men work together.

OEDIPUS Children, poor helpless children,
         I know what brings you here, I know.   80
         You suffer, this plague is agony for each of you,
         but none of you, not one suffers as I do.
         Each of you suffers for himself, only himself.
         My whole being wails and breaks
         for this city, for myself, for all of you,
         old man, all of you.
         Everything ends here, with me. I am the man.
         You have not wakened me from some kind of sleep.
         I have wept, struggled, wandered in this maze of thought,
         tried every road, searched hard—   90
         finally I found one cure, only one:
         I sent my wife's brother, Kreon, to great Apollo's shrine at
              Delphi;
         I sent him to learn what I must say or do to save Thebes.
         But his long absence troubles me. Why isn't he here?
              Where is he?
         When he returns, what kind of man would I be
         if I failed to do everything the god reveals?

         *Some of the suppliants by the steps to the orchestra stand
         to announce* KREON's *arrival to the* PRIEST. KREON *comes in
         by the entrance to the audience's left with a garland on his
         head.*

PRIEST   You speak of Kreon, and Kreon is here.

OEDIPUS *(turning to the altar of Apollo, then to* KREON*)*
         Lord Apollo, look at him—his head is crowned with laurel, his
              eyes glitter.
         Let his words blaze, blaze like his eyes, and save us.

PRIEST   He looks calm, radiant, like a god. If he brought bad news,   100
         would he be wearing that crown of sparkling leaves?

OEDIPUS At last we will know.
         Lord Kreon, what did the god Apollo say?

KREON His words are hopeful.
　　　　Once everything is clear, exposed to the light,
　　　　we will see our suffering is blessing. All we need is luck.

OEDIPUS What do you mean? What did Apollo say? What should
　　　　　　we do?
　　　　　Speak.

KREON Here? Now? In front of all these people?
　　　　Or inside, privately?   110

　　　　　　　　　　　　　　KREON moves toward the palace.

OEDIPUS Stop. Say it. Say it to the whole city.
　　　　　I grieve for them, for their sorrow and loss, far more than I
　　　　　　　grieve for myself.

KREON This is what I heard—there was no mistaking the god's
　　　　　　meaning—
　　　　Apollo commands us:
　　　　Cleanse the city of Thebes, cleanse the plague from that city,
　　　　destroy the black stain spreading everywhere, spreading,
　　　　poisoning the earth, touching each house, each citizen,
　　　　sickening the hearts of the people of Thebes!
　　　　Cure this disease that wastes all of you, spreading, spreading,
　　　　before it grows so vast nothing can cure it   120

OEDIPUS What is this plague?
　　　　　How can we purify the city?

KREON A man must be banished. Banished or killed.
　　　　Blood for blood. The plague is blood,
　　　　blood, breaking over Thebes.

OEDIPUS Who is the man? Who is Apollo's victim?

KREON My lord, before you came to Thebes, before you came to
　　　　　　power,
　　　　Laios was our king.

OEDIPUS   I know. But I never saw Laios.

KREON   Laios was murdered. Apollo's command was very clear: 130
Avenge the murderers of Laios. Whoever they are.

OEDIPUS   But where are his murderers?
The crime is old. How will we find their tracks?
The killers could be anywhere.

KREON   Apollo said the killers are still here, here in Thebes.
Pursue a thing, and you may catch it;
ignored, it slips away.

OEDIPUS   And Laios—where was he murdered?
At home? Or was he away from Thebes?

KREON   He told us before he left—he was on a mission to Delphi,   140
his last trip away from Thebes. He never returned.

OEDIPUS   Wasn't there a witness, someone with Laios who saw what
happened?

KREON   They were all killed, except for one man. He escaped.
But he was so terrified he remembered only one thing.

OEDIPUS   What was it? One small clue might lead to others.

KREON   This is what he said: bandits ambushed Laios, not one man.
They attacked him like hail crushing a stalk of wheat.

OEDIPUS   How could a single bandit dare attack a king
unless he had supporters, people with money, here,
here in Thebes?   150

KREON   There were suspicions. But after Laios died we had no
leader, no king.
Our life was turmoil, uncertainty.

OEDIPUS But once the throne was empty,
        what threw you off the track, what kept you from searching
        until you uncovered everything, knew every detail?

KREON The intricate, hard song of the Sphinx
        persuaded us the crime was not important, not then.
        It seemed to say we should focus on what lay at our feet, in
            front of us,
        ignore what we could not see.

OEDIPUS Now *I* am here.   160
        I will begin the search again, I
        will reveal the truth, expose everything, let it all be seen.
        Apollo and you were right to make us wonder about the
            dead man.
        Like Apollo, I am your ally.
        Justice and vengeance are what I want,
        for Thebes, for the god.
        Family, friends—I won't rid myself of this stain, this disease,
            for them—
        they're far from here. I'll do it for myself, for me.
        The man who killed Laios might take revenge on me
        just as violently.   170
        So by avenging Laios' death, I protect myself.
        (*turning to the suppliants*) Rise, children,
        pick up your branches,
        let someone announce my decision to the whole city of
            Thebes.
        (*to the Priest*) I will do everything. Everything.
        And, with the god's help, we will be saved.
        Bright Apollo, let your light help us see.
        Our happiness is yours to give, our failure and ruin yours.

PRIEST Rise. We have the help we came for, children.
        The king himself has promised.   180
        May Apollo, who gave these oracles, come as our savior now.
        Apollo, heal us, save us from this plague!

OEDIPUS enters the palace. Its doors close. KREON leaves by a door to the right on the wing of the stage. The PRIEST and suppliants go down into the orchestra and leave by the entrance to the left as a chorus of fifteen Theban elders files into the orchestra by the entrance on the right, preceded by a flute player.

CHORUS voice   voice   voice
        voice who knows everything o god
        glorious voice of Zeus
        how have you come from Delphi bathed in gold
        what are you telling our bright city Thebes
        what are you bringing me
        health death fear
        I know nothing   190
        so frightened rooted here
        awed by you
        healer what have you sent
        is it the sudden doom of grief
        or the old curse the darkness
        looming in the turning season

        o holy immortal voice
        hope golden seed of the future
        listen be with me speak
        these cries of mine rise   200
        tell me
        I call to you reach out to you first
        holy Athena god's daughter who lives forever
        and your sister Artemis
        who cradles the earth our earth
        who sits on her great throne at the hub of the market place
        and I call to Apollo who hurls light
        from deep in the sky
        o gods be with us now
        shine on us your three shields   210
        blazing against the darkness
        come in our suffering as you came once before
        to Thebes o bright divinities

and threw your saving light against the god of grief
o gods
be with us now

pain pain my sorrows have no sound
no name no word no pain like this
plague sears my people everywhere
everyone army citizens no one escapes   220
no spear of strong anxious thought protects us
great Thebes grows nothing
seeds rot in the ground
our women when they labor
cry Apollo Apollo but their children die
and lives one after another split the air
birds taking off
wingrush hungrier than fire
souls leaping away they fly
to the shore   230
of the cold god of evening
west

the death stain spreads
so many corpses lie in the streets everywhere
nobody grieves for them
the city dies and young wives
and mothers gray-haired mothers wail
sob on the altar steps
they come from the city everywhere mourning their bit-
    ter days
prayers blaze to the Healer   240
grief cries a flute mingling
daughter of Zeus o shining daughter show us
the warm bright face of peace of help
of our salvation

                    The doors of the palace open. OEDIPUS *enters.*

and turn back the huge raging jaws of the death god Ares
drive him back drive him away

his flames lash at me
this is his war these are his shields
shouts pierce us on all sides
turn him back lift him on a strong wind   250
rush him away
to the two seas at the world's edge
the sea where the waters boil
the sea where no traveler can land
because if night leaves anything alive
day destroys it
o Zeus
god beyond all other gods
handler of the fire
father   260
make the god of our sickness
ashes

Apollo
great bowman of light draw back your bow
fire arrow after arrow
make them a wall circling us
shoot into our enemy's eyes
draw the string twined with gold
come goddess
who dances on the mountains   270
sowing light where your feet brush the ground
blind our enemy come
god of golden hair
piled under your golden cap Bacchus
your face blazing like the sea when the sun falls on it
like sunlight on wine
god whose name is our name Bacchus
god of joy god of terror
be with us now your bright face
like a pine torch roaring   280
thrust into the face of the slaughtering war god
blind him
drive him down from Olympos

drive him away from Thebes
forever

OEDIPUS Every word of your prayers has touched me.
          Listen. Follow me. Join me in fighting this sickness, this
                plague,
          and all your sufferings may end, like a dark sky,
          clear suddenly, blue, after a week of storms,
          soothing the torn face of the sea,   290
          soothing our fears.
          Your fate looms in my words—
          I heard nothing about Laios' death,
          I know nothing about the murder,
          I was alone, how could I have tracked the killer, without a
                clue,
          I came to Thebes after the crime was done,
          I was made a Theban after Laios' death. Listen carefully—
          these words come from an innocent man.

                              Addressing the CHORUS.

          One of you knows who killed Laios.
          Where is that man?   300
          Speak.
          I command it. Fear is no excuse.
          He must clear himself of the dangerous charge.
          Who did this thing?
          Was it a stranger?
          Speak.
          I will not harm him. The worst he will suffer is exile.
          I will pay him well. He will have a king's thanks.
          But if he will not speak because he fears me,
          if he fears what I will do to him or to those he loves,   310
          if he will not obey me,
          I say to him:
          My power is absolute in Thebes, my rule reaches everywhere,
          my words will drive the guilty man, the man who knows,
          out of this city, away from Thebes, forever.

Nothing.
My word for him is nothing.
Let him *be* nothing.
Give him nothing.
Let him touch nothing of yours, he is nothing to you.   320
Lock your doors when he approaches.
Say nothing to him, do not speak.
No prayers with him, no offerings with him.
No purifying water.
Nothing.
Drive him from your homes. Let him have no home,
     nothing.
No words, no food, shelter, warmth of hand, shared worship.
Let him have nothing. Drive him out, let him die.
He is our disease.

                    I know.   330
                              Apollo has made it clear.
Nothing can stop me, nothing can change my words.
I fight for Apollo, I fight for the dead man.
You see me, you hear me, moving against the killer.
My words are his doom.
Whether he did it alone, and escaped unseen,
whether others helped him kill, it makes no difference—
let my hatred burn out his life, hatred, always.
Make him an ember of suffering.
Make all his happiness   340
ashes.
If he eats at my side, sits at my sacred hearth, and I know
     these things,
let every curse I spit out against him find *me*,
come home to *me*.
Carry out my orders. You must,
for me, for Apollo, and for Thebes, Thebes,
this poor wasted city,
deserted by its gods.
I know—the gods have given us this disease.   350
That makes no difference. You should have acted,
you should have done something long ago to purge our guilt.

The victim was noble, a king—
you should have done everything to track his murderer down.
And so,
because I rule now where he ruled;
because I share his bed, his wife;
because the same woman who mothered my children might
    have mothered his;
because fate swooped out of nowhere and cut him down;
because of all these things   360
I will fight for him as I would fight for my own murdered
    father.
Nothing will stop me.
No man, no place, nothing will escape my gaze. I will not
    stop
until I know it all, all, until everything is clear.
For every king, every king's son and his sons,
for every royal generation of Thebes, my Thebes,
I will expose the killer, I will reveal him
to the light.
Oh gods, gods,
destroy all those who will not listen, will not obey.   370
Freeze the ground until they starve.
Make their wives barren as stone.
Let this disease that shakes Thebes to its roots—
or any worse disease, if there is any worse than this—waste
    them,
crush everything they have, everything they are.
But you men of Thebes—
you, who know my words are right, who obey me—
may justice and the gods defend you, bless you,
graciously, forever.

LEADER Your curse forces me to speak, Master.   380
        I cannot escape it.
        I did not murder the king, I cannot show you the man who
           did.
        Apollo told us to search for the killer.
        Apollo must name him.

OEDIPUS No man can force the gods to speak.

LEADER Then I will say the next best thing.

OEDIPUS If there's a third best thing, say that too.

LEADER Teiresias sees what the god Apollo sees.
Truth, truth.
If you heard the god speaking, heard his voice,   390
you might see more, more, and more.

OEDIPUS Teiresias? I have seen to that already.
Kreon spoke of Teiresias, and I sent for him. Twice.
I find it strange he still hasn't come.

LEADER And there's an old story, almost forgotten,
a dark, faded rumor.

OEDIPUS What rumor? I must sift each story,
see it, understand it.

LEADER Laios was killed by bandits.

OEDIPUS I have heard that story: but who can show me the man who   400
saw the murderer?
Has anyone seen him?

LEADER If he knows the meaning of fear,
if he heard those curses you spoke against him,
those words still scorching the air,
you won't find him now, not in Thebes.

OEDIPUS The man murdered. Why would words frighten him?

TEIRESIAS *has appeared from the stage entrance to the right
of the audience. He walks with a staff and is helped by a
slave boy and attendants. He stops at some distance from
center stage.*

LEADER Here is the man who can catch the criminal.
They're bringing him now—
the godlike prophet who speaks with the voice of god.
He, only he, knows truth.   410
The truth is rooted in his soul.

OEDIPUS Teiresias, you understand all things,
what can be taught, what is locked in silence,
the distant things of heaven, and things that crawl the earth.
You cannot see, yet you know the nature of this plague in-
       festing our city.
Only you, my lord, can save us, only you can defend us.
Apollo told our messenger—did you hear?—
that we could be saved only by tracking down Laios' killers,
only by killing them, or sending them into exile.
Help us, Teiresias.   420
Study the cries of birds, study their wild paths,
ponder the signs of fire, use all your skills of prophecy.
Rescue us, preserve us.
Rescue yourself, rescue Thebes, rescue me.
Cleanse every trace of the growing stain left by the dead
       man's blood.
We are in your hands, Teiresias.
No work is more nobly human than helping others,
helping with all the strength and skill we possess.

TEIRESIAS Wisdom is a curse
when wisdom does nothing for the man who has it.   430
Once I knew this well, but I forgot.
I never should have come.

OEDIPUS Never should have come? Why this reluctance, prophet?

TEIRESIAS Let me go home.
That way is best, for you, for me.
Let me live my life, and you live yours.

OEDIPUS Strange words, Teiresias, cruel to the city that gave you life.

Your holy knowledge could save Thebes. How can you keep
   silent?

TEIRESIAS What have you said that helps Thebes? Your words are
   wasted.
   I would rather be silent than waste my words.   440

OEDIPUS Look at us,   (OEDIPUS *stands, the* CHORUS *kneel*)
   kneeling to you, Teiresias, imploring you.
   In the name of the gods, if you know—
   help us, tell us what you know.

TEIRESIAS You kneel because you do not understand.
   But I will never let you see my grief. Never.
   My grief is yours.

OEDIPUS What? You know and won't speak?
   You'd betray us all, you'd destroy the city of Thebes?

TEIRESIAS I will do nothing to hurt myself, or you. Why insist?   450
   I will not speak.

OEDIPUS Stubborn old fool, you'd make a rock angry!
   Tell me what you know! Say it!
   Where are your feelings? Won't you ever speak?

TEIRESIAS You call me cold, stubborn, unfeeling, you insult me. But
      you,
   Oedipus, what do you know about yourself,
   about your real feelings?
   You don't see how much alike we are.

OEDIPUS How can *I* restrain my anger when I see how little you care
   for Thebes.

TEIRESIAS The truth will come, by itself,   460
   the truth will come
   no matter how I shroud it in silence.

OEDIPUS All the more reason why you should speak.

TEIRESIAS Not another word.
Rage away. You will never make me speak.

OEDIPUS I'll rage, prophet, I'll give you all my anger.
I'll say it all—
Listen: I think you were involved in the murder of Laios,
you helped plan it, I think you
did everything in your power to kill Laios,   470
everything but strike him with your own hands,
and if you weren't blind, if you still had eyes to see with,
I'd say you, and you alone, did it all.

TEIRESIAS Do you think so? Then obey your own words, obey
the curse everyone heard break from your own lips:
Never speak again to these men of Thebes,
never speak again to me.
                              You, it's
you.   480
What plagues the city is you.
The plague is you.

OEDIPUS Do you know what you're saying?
Do you think I'll let you get away with these vile accusations?

TEIRESIAS I am safe.
Truth lives in me, and the truth is strong.

OEDIPUS Who taught you this truth of yours? Not your prophet's
craft.

TEIRESIAS You taught me. You forced me to speak.

OEDIPUS Speak what? Explain. Teach me.

TEIRESIAS Didn't you understand?
Are you trying to make me say the word?   490

OEDIPUS   What word? Say it. Spit it out.

TEIRESIAS   Murderer.
            I say you,
            you are the killer you're searching for.

OEDIPUS   You won't say *that* again to me and get away with it.

TEIRESIAS   Do you want more? Shall I make you really angry?

OEDIPUS   Say anything you like. Your words are wasted.

TEIRESIAS   I say you live in shame, and you do not know it,
            do not know that you
            and those you love most   500
            wallow in shame,
            you do not know
            in what shame you live.

OEDIPUS   You'll pay for these insults, I swear it.

TEIRESIAS   Not if the truth is strong.

OEDIPUS   The truth *is* strong, but not your truth.
          You have no truth. You're blind.
          Blind in your eyes. Blind in your ears. Blind in your mind.

TEIRESIAS   And I pity you for mocking my blindness.
            Soon everyone in Thebes will mock you, Oedipus. They'll   510
               mock you
            as you have mocked me.

OEDIPUS   One endless night swaddles you in its unbroken black sky.
          You can't hurt me, you can't hurt anyone who sees the light
             of day.

TEIRESIAS   True. Nothing I do will harm you. You, you
            and your fate belong to Apollo.
            Apollo will see to you.

OEDIPUS Are these your own lies, prophet—or Kreon's?

TEIRESIAS Kreon? Your plague is you, not Kreon.

OEDIPUS Money, power, one great skill surpassing another,
if a man has these things, other men's envy grows and grows,   520
their greed and hunger are insatiable.
Most men would lust for a life like mine—but I did not
    demand my life,
Thebes gave me my life, and from the beginning, my good
    friend Kreon,
loyal, trusted Kreon,
was reaching for my power, wanted to ambush me, get rid of
    me by hiring this cheap wizard,
this crass, conniving priest, who sees nothing but profit,
whose prophecy is simple profit. You,
what did you ever do that proves you a real seer? What did
    you ever see, prophet?
And when the Sphinx who sang mysteriously   530
imprisoned us
why didn't you speak and set us free?
No ordinary man could have solved her riddle,
it took prophecy, prophecy and skill you clearly never had.
Even the paths of birds, even the gods' voices were useless.
But I showed up, I, Oedipus,
stupid, untutored Oedipus,
I silenced her, I destroyed her, I used my wits, not omens,
to sift the meaning of her song.
And this is the man you want to kill so you can get close to   540
    King Kreon,
weigh his affairs for him, advise him, influence him.
No, I think you and your master, Kreon, who contrived this
    plot,
will be whipped out of Thebes.
Look at you.
If you weren't so old, and weak, oh
I'd make you pay
for this conspiracy of yours.

LEADER   Oedipus, both of you spoke in anger.

Anger is not what we need.

We need all our wits, all our energy to interpret Apollo's 550
words.

Then we will know what to do.

TEIRESIAS   Oedipus, you are king, but you must hear my reply.

My right to speak is just as valid as yours.

I am not your slave. Kreon is not my patron.

My master is Apollo. I can say what I please.

You insulted me. You mocked me. You called me blind.

Now hear me speak, Oedipus.

You have eyes to see with,

but you do not see yourself, you do not see

the horror shadowing every step of your life, 560

the blind shame in which you live,

you do not see where you live and who lives with you,

lives always at your side.

Tell me, Oedipus, who are your parents?

Do you know?

You do not even know

the shame and grief you have brought your family,

those still alive, those buried beneath the earth.

But the curse of your mother, the curse of your father

will whip you, whip you again and again, wherever you turn, 570

it will whip you out of Thebes forever,

your clear eyes flooded with darkness.

That day will come.

And then what scoured, homeless plain, what leafless tree,

what place on Kithairon,

where no other humans are or ever will be,

where the wind is the only thing that moves,

what raw track of thorns and stones, what rock, gulley,

or blind hill won't echo your screams, your howls of anguish

when you find out that the marriage song, 580

sung when you came to Thebes, heard in your house,

guided you to this shore, this wilderness

you thought was home, your home?

And you do not see
all the other awful things
that will show you who you really are, show you
to your children, face to face.
Go ahead! Call me quack, abuse Kreon, insult Apollo, the god
who speaks through me, whose words move on my lips.
No man will ever know worse suffering than you,   590
your life, your flesh, your happiness an ember of pain. Ashes.

OEDIPUS (*to the* CHORUS) Must I stand here and listen to these
       attacks?

TEIRESIAS (*beginning to move away*) I am here, Oedipus, because you
       sent for me.

OEDIPUS You old fool,
       I'd have thought twice before asking you to come
       if I had known you'd spew out such idiocy.

TEIRESIAS Call me fool, if you like, but your parents,
       who gave you life, they respected my judgment.

OEDIPUS Parents?
             What do you mean?   600
                         Who are my mother and father?

TEIRESIAS This day is your mother and father—this day will give you
       your birth,
       it will destroy you too.

OEDIPUS How you love mysterious, twisted words.

TEIRESIAS Aren't you the great solver of riddles?
       Aren't you Oedipus?

OEDIPUS Taunt me for the gift of my brilliant mind.
       That gift is what makes me great.

TEIRESIAS That gift is your destiny. It made you everything you are,
and it has ruined you.   610

OEDIPUS But if this gift of mine saved Thebes, who cares what happens to me?

TEIRESIAS I'm leaving. Boy, take me home.

OEDIPUS Good. Take him home. Here
I keep stumbling over you, here you're in my way.
Scuttle home, and leave us in peace!

TEIRESIAS I'm going. I said what I came to say,
and that scowl, darkening your face, doesn't frighten me.
How can you hurt me?
I tell you again:
the man you've been trying to expose—
with all your threats, with your inquest into Laios' murder—   620
that man is here, in Thebes.
Now people think he comes from Corinth, but later
they will see he was born in Thebes.
When they know, he'll have no pleasure in that news.
Now he has eyes to see with, but they will be slashed out;
rich and powerful now, he will be a beggar,
poking his way with a stick, feeling his way to a strange
country.
And his children—the children he lives with—
will see him at last, see what he is, see who he really is:
their brother and their father; his wife's son, his mother's   630
husband;
the lover who slept with his father's wife; the man who murdered his father—
the man whose hands still drip with his father's blood.
These truths will be revealed.

Go inside and ponder *that* riddle, and if you find I've lied,
then call me a prophet who cannot see.

OEDIPUS turns and enters the palace. TEIRESIAS *is led out*
                    through the stage entrance on the right.

CHORUS   who did crimes unnameable things
            things words cringe at
            which man did the rock of prophecy at Delphi say
            did these things
            his hands dripping with blood   640
            he should run now flee
            his strong feet swallowing the air
            stronger than the horses of storm winds
            their hooves slicing the air
            now in his armor
            Apollo lunges at him
            his infinite branching fire reaches out
            and the steady dread death-hungry Fates follow and never
                stop
            their quick scissors seeking the cloth of his life

                                                                    650
            just now
            from high snowy Parnassus
            the god's voice exploded its blazing message
            follow his track find the man
            no one knows
            a bull loose under wild bushes and trees
            among caves and gray rocks
            cut from the herd he runs and runs but runs nowhere
            zigzagging desperate to get away
            birds of prophecy birds of death circling his head
            forever   660
            voices forged at the white stone core of the earth
            they go where he goes always

            terror's in me flooding me
            how can I judge
            what the god Apollo says
            trapped hoping confused
            I do not see what is here now

when I look to the past I see nothing
I know nothing about a feud
wounding the families of Laios or Oedipus   670
no clue to the truth then or now
nothing to blacken his golden fame in Thebes
and help Laios' family
solve the mystery of his death

Zeus and Apollo know
they understand
only they see
the dark threads crossing beneath our life
but no man can say a prophet sees more than I
one man surpasses another   680
wisdom against wisdom skill against skill
but I will not blame Oedipus
whatever anyone says
until words are as real as things

one thing is clear
years back the Sphinx tested him
his answer was true
he was wise and sweet to the city
so he can never be evil
not to me   690

KREON *enters through the stage entrance at right, and ad-*
dresses the CHORUS.

KREON Men of Thebes, I hear Oedipus, our king and master,
has brought terrible charges against me.
I have come to face those charges. I resent them bitterly.
If he imagines I have hurt him, spoken or acted against him
while our city dies, believe me—I have nothing left to live for.
His accusations pierce me, wound me mortally—
nothing they touch is trivial, private—
if you, my family and friends,
think I'm a traitor, if all Thebes believes it, says it.

LEADER Perhaps he spoke in anger, without thinking,   700
       perhaps his anger made him accuse you.

KREON Did he really say I persuaded Teiresias to lie?

LEADER I heard him say these things,
       but I don't know what they mean.

KREON Did he look you in the eyes when he accused me?
       Was he in his right mind?

LEADER I do not know or see what great men do.

          (turning to OEDIPUS, who has emerged from the palace)

       But here he is—Oedipus.

OEDIPUS What? You here? Murderer!
       You dare come here, to my palace, when it's clear   710
       you've been plotting to murder me and seize the throne of
          Thebes?
       You're the bandit, you're the killer.
                            Answer me—
       Did you think I was cowardly or stupid?
       Is that why you betrayed me?
       Did you really think I wouldn't see wnat you were plotting,
       how you crept up on me like a cloud inching across the sun?
       Did you think I wouldn't defend myself against you?
       You thought I was a fool, but the fool was you, Kreon.
       Thrones are won with money and men, you fool!   720

KREON You have said enough, Oedipus. Now let me reply.
       Weigh my words against your charges, then judge for your-
          self.

OEDIPUS Eloquent, Kreon. But you won't convince me now.
       Now that I know your hatred, your malice.

KREON   Let me explain.

OEDIPUS Explain?
         What could explain your treachery?

KREON   If you think this stubborn anger of yours, this perversity,
         is something to be proud of, you're mad.

OEDIPUS And if you think you can injure your sister's husband,   730
         and not pay for it, you're mad.

KREON   I would be mad to hurt you. How have I hurt you?

OEDIPUS Was it you who advised me to send for that great holy
         prophet?

KREON   Yes, and I'd do it again.

OEDIPUS How long has it been since Laios disappeared?

KREON   Disappeared?

OEDIPUS Died. Was murdered. . . .

KREON   Many, many years.

OEDIPUS And this prophet of yours—was he practicing his trade at the
         time?

KREON   With as much skill, wisdom and honor as ever.   740

OEDIPUS Did he ever mention my name?

KREON   Not in my presence.

OEDIPUS Was there an inquest? A formal inquiry?

KREON   Of course. Nothing was ever discovered.

OEDIPUS Then why didn't our wonderful prophet, our Theban wizard,
         denounce me as the murderer then?

KREON I don't know. And when I don't know, I don't speak.

OEDIPUS But you know this. You know it with perfect certainty.

KREON What do you mean?

OEDIPUS This: if you and Teiresias were not conspiring against me,   750
         Teiresias would never have charged me with Laios' murder.

KREON If he said that, you should know.
       But now, Oedipus it's my right, my turn to question you.

OEDIPUS Ask anything. You'll never prove I killed Laios.

KREON Did you marry my sister, Jocasta?

OEDIPUS I married Jocasta.

KREON And you gave her an equal share of the power in Thebes?

OEDIPUS Whatever she wants is hers.

KREON And I share that power equally with you and her?

OEDIPUS Equally.   760
         And that's precisely why it's clear you're false, treacherous.

KREON No, Oedipus.
       Consider it rationally, as I have. Reflect:
       What man, what sane man, would prefer a king's power
       with all its dangers and anxieties,
       when he could enjoy that same power, without its cares,
       and sleep in peace each night? Power?
       I have no instinct for power, no hunger for it either.

It isn't royal power I want, but its advantages.
And any sensible man would want the same.   770
Look at the life I lead. Whatever I want, I get from you,
with your goodwill and blessing. I have nothing to fear.
If I were king, my life would be constant duty and constraint.
Why would I want your power or the throne of Thebes
more than what I enjoy now—the privilege of power
without its dangers? I would be a fool to want more
than what I have—the substance, not the show, of power.
As matters stand, no man envies me, I am courted
and admired by all. Men wear no smiling masks for Kreon.
And those who want something from you come to me   780
because the way to royal favor lies through me.
Tell me, Oedipus, why should I give these blessings up
to seize your throne and all the dangers it confers?
A man like me, who knows his mortal limits and accepts
        them,
cannot be vicious or treacherous by nature.
The love of power is not my nature, nor is treason
or the thoughts of treason that go with love of power.
I would never dare conspire against your life.

Do you want to test the truth of what I say?
Go to Delphi, put the question to the oracle,   790
ask if I have told you exactly what Apollo said.
Then if you find that Teiresias and I have plotted against
        you,
seize me and put me to death. Convict me
not by one vote alone, but two—yours and mine, Oedipus.
But don't convict me on the strength of your suspicions,
don't confuse friends with traitors, traitors with friends.
There's no justice in that.
To throw away a good and loyal friend
is to destroy what you love most—
your own life, and what makes life worth living.   800
Someday you will know the truth:
time, only time reveals the good man;
one day's light reveals the evil man.

LEADER   Good words
         for someone careful, afraid he'll fall.
         But a mind like lightning
         stumbles.

OEDIPUS When a clever man plots against me and moves swiftly
         I must move just as swiftly, I must plan.
         But if I wait, if I do nothing, he will win, win everything,   810
         and I will lose.

KREON   What do you want? My exile?

OEDIPUS No. Your death.

KREON   You won't change your mind? You won't believe me?

OEDIPUS I'll believe you when you teach me the meaning of envy.

KREON   Envy? You talk about envy. You don't even know what
             sense is.
         Can't you listen to me?

OEDIPUS I am listening. To my own good sense.

KREON   Listen to me. I have sense on my side too.

OEDIPUS You? You were born devious.   820

KREON   And if you're wrong?

OEDIPUS I still must govern.

KREON   Not if you govern badly.

OEDIPUS Oh Thebes, Thebes . . .

KREON   Thebes is mine too.

LEADER (*turning to* JOCASTA, *who has entered from the palace, accompanied by a woman attendant*)
Stop. I see
Jocasta coming from the palace
just in time, my lords, to help you
settle this deep, bitter feud raging between you.
Listen to what she says.   830

JOCASTA Oedipus! Kreon! Why this insane quarreling?
You should be ashamed, both of you. Forget yourselves.
This is no time for petty personal bickering.
Thebes is sick, dying.
                   —Come inside, Oedipus
—And you, Kreon, leave us.
Must you create all this misery over nothing, nothing?

KRÉON Jocasta,
Oedipus has given me two impossible choices:
Either I must be banished from Thebes, my city, my home,   840
or be arrested and put to death.

OEDIPUS That's right.
I caught him plotting against me, Jocasta.
Viciously, cunningly plotting against the king of Thebes.

KREON Take every pleasure I have in life, curse me, let me die,
if I've done what you accuse me of, let the gods
destroy everything I have, let them do anything to me.
I stand here, exposed to their infinite power.

JOCASTA Oedipus, in the name of the gods, believe him.
His prayer has made him holy, naked to the mysterious   850
whims of the gods, has taken him beyond what is human.
Respect his words, respect me, respect these men standing at
      your side.

CHORUS (*beginning a dirge-like appeal to* OEDIPUS)
listen to her

          think yield
          we implore you

OEDIPUS What do you want?

CHORUS be generous to Kreon give him respect
          he was never foolish before
          now his prayer to the gods has made him great
          great and frightening   860

OEDIPUS Do you know what you're asking?

CHORUS I know

OEDIPUS Then say it.

CHORUS don't ever cut him off
          without rights or honor
          blood binds you both
          his prayer has made him sacred
          don't accuse him
          because some blind suspicion hounds you

OEDIPUS Understand me: 870
          when you ask for these things
          you ask for my death or exile.

CHORUS no
          by the sun
          the god who bathes us in his light
          who sees all
          I will die godless no family no friends
          if what I ask means that
          it is Thebes
          Thebes dying wasting away life by life   880
          this is the misery
          that breaks my heart

53

and now this quarrel raging between you and Kreon
is more more than I can bear

OEDIPUS Then let him go, even if it means I must die
or be forced out of Thebes forever, stripped of all my rights,
     all my honors.
Your grief, your words touch me. Not his.
I pity you. But him,
my hatred will reach him wherever he goes.

KREON It's clear you hate to yield, clear   890
you yield only under pressure, only
when you've worn out the fierceness of your anger.
Then all you can do is sit, and brood.
Natures like yours are a torment to themselves.

OEDIPUS Leave. Go!

KREON I'm going. Now I know
you do not know me.
But these men know I am the man I seem to be, a just man,
not devious, not a traitor.

                                   KREON *leaves.*

CHORUS woman why are you waiting   900
lead him inside comfort him

JOCASTA Not before I know what has happened here.

CHORUS blind ignorant words suspicion without proof
the injustice of it
gnaws at us

JOCASTA From both men?

CHORUS yes

JOCASTA What caused it?

CHORUS enough enough
        no more words   910
        Thebes is so tormented now
        let it rest where it ended

OEDIPUS Look where cooling my rage,
         where all your decent, practical thoughts have led you.

CHORUS Oedipus I have said this many times
        I would be mad helpless to give advice
        if I turned against you now
        once
        you took our city in her storm of pain
        straightened her course found fair weather   920
        o lead her to safety now
        if you can

JOCASTA If you love the gods, tell me, too, Oedipus—I implore you—
         why are you still so angry, why can't you let it go?

OEDIPUS I will tell you, Jocasta.
         You mean more, far more to me than these men here.
         Jocasta, it is Kreon—Kreon and his plots against me.

JOCASTA What started your quarrel?

OEDIPUS He said I murdered Laios.

JOCASTA Does he know something? Or is it pure hearsay?   930

OEDIPUS He sent me a vicious, trouble-making prophet
         to avoid implicating himself. He did not say it to my face.

JOCASTA Oedipus, forget all this. Listen to me:
         no mortal can practise the art of prophecy, no man can see
              the future.
         One experience of mine will show you why.
         Long ago an oracle came to Laios.
         It came not from Apollo himself but from his priests.

It said Laios was doomed to be murdered by a son, his son
    and mine.
But Laios, from what we heard, was murdered by bandits
    from a foreign country,
cut down at a crossroads. My poor baby   940
was only three days old when Laios had his feet pierced to-
    gether behind the ankles
and gave orders to abandon our child on a mountain, leave
    him alone to die
in a wilderness of rocks and bare gray trees
where there were no roads, no people.
So you see—Apollo didn't make that child his father's killer,
Laios wasn't murdered by his son. That dreadful act which
    so terrified Laios—
it never happened.

All those oracular voices meant was nothing, nothing.
Ignore them.
Apollo creates. Apollo reveals. He needs no help from men.   950

OEDIPUS (who has been very still)
    While you were speaking, Jocasta, it flashed through my
        mind
like wind suddenly ruffling a stretch of calm sea.
It stuns me. I can almost see it—some memory, some image.
My heart races and swells—

JOCASTA Why are you so strangely excited, Oedipus?

OEDIPUS You said Laios was cut down near a crossroads?

JOCASTA That was the story. It hasn't changed.

OEDIPUS Where did it happen? Tell me. Where?

JOCASTA In Phokis. Where the roads from Delphi and Daulia meet.

OEDIPUS When?   960

JOCASTA Just before you came to Thebes and assumed power.
Just before you were proclaimed King.

OEDIPUS O Zeus, Zeus,
what are you doing with my life?

JOCASTA Why are you so disturbed, Oedipus?

OEDIPUS Don't ask me. Not yet.
Tell me about Laios.
How old was he? What did he look like?

JOCASTA Streaks of gray were beginning to show in his black hair.
He was tall, strong—built something like you.   970

OEDIPUS No! O gods, o
it seems each hard, arrogant curse
I spit out
was meant for me, and I
didn't
know it!

JOCASTA Oedipus, what do you mean? Your face is so strange.
You frighten me.

OEDIPUS It is frightening—can the blind prophet see, can he really see?
I would know if you told me . . .   980

JOCASTA I'm afraid to ask, Oedipus.
Told you what?

OEDIPUS Was Laios traveling with a small escort
or with many armed men, like a king?

JOCASTA There were five, including a herald.
Laios was riding in his chariot.

OEDIPUS Light, o light, light
now everything, everything is clear. All of it.
Who told you this? Who was it?

JOCASTA   A household slave. The only survivor.   990

OEDIPUS   Is he here, in Thebes?

JOCASTA   No. When he returned and saw that you were king
          and learned Laios was dead, he came to me and clutched my
              hand,
          begged me to send him to the mountains
          where shepherds graze their flocks, far from the city,
          so he could never see Thebes again.
          I sent him, of course. He deserved that much, for a slave,
              and more.

OEDIPUS   Can he be called back? Now?

JOCASTA   Easily. But why?

OEDIPUS   I am afraid I may have said too much—   1000
          I must see him.
          Now.

JOCASTA   Then he will come.
          But surely I have a right to know what disturbs you, Oedipus.

OEDIPUS   Now that I've come this far, Jocasta,
          hope torturing me, each step of mine heavy with fear,
          I won't keep anything from you.
          Wandering through the mazes of a fate like this,
          how could I confide in anyone but you?

          My father was Polybos, of Corinth.   1010
          My mother, Merope, was Dorian.
          Everyone in Corinth saw me as its first citizen,
          but one day something happened,
          something strange, puzzling. Puzzling, but nothing more.
          Still, it worried me.
          One night, I was at a banquet,

and a man—he was very drunk—said I wasn't my father's son,
called me "bastard." That stung me, I was shocked.
I could barely control my anger, I lay awake all night.
The next day I went to my father and mother,   1020
I questioned them about the man and what he said.
They were furious with him, outraged by his insult,
and I was reassured. But I kept hearing the word "bastard"
        "bastard"—
I couldn't get it out of my head.
Without my parents' knowledge, I went to Delphi: I
        wanted the truth,
but Apollo refused to answer me.
And yet he did reveal other things, he did show me
a future dark with torment, evil, horror,
he made me see—
see myself, doomed to sleep with my own mother, doomed   1030
to bring children into this world where the sun pours down,
children no one could bear to see, doomed
to murder the man who gave me life, whose blood is my
        blood. My father.
And after I heard all this, I fled Corinth,
measuring my progress by the stars, searching for a place
where I would never see those words, those dreadful predic-
        tions
come true. And on my way
I came to the place where you say King Laios was murdered.

Jocasta, the story I'm about to tell you is the truth:
I was on the road, near the crossroads you mentioned,   1040
when I met a herald, with an old man, just as you
        described him.
The man was riding in a chariot
and his driver tried to push me off the road
and when he shoved me I hit him. I hit him.
The old man stood quiet in the chariot until I passed under
        him,
then he leaned out and caught me on the head with an ugly
        goad—

its two teeth wounded me—and with this hand of mine,
this hand clenched around my staff,
I struck him back even harder—so hard, so quick he couldn't
    dodge it,
and he toppled out of the chariot and hit the ground, face   1050
    up.
I killed them. Every one of them. I still see them.

                       (*to the* CHORUS)

If this stranger and Laios
are somehow linked by blood,
tell me what man's torment equals mine?

Citizens, hear my curse again—
Give this man nothing. Let him touch nothing of yours.
Lock your doors when he approaches.
Say nothing to him when he approaches.
                  And these, these curses,
with my own mouth I   1060
spoke these monstrous curses against myself.

             (OEDIPUS *turns back to* JOCASTA)

These hands, these bloodstained hands made love to you in
    your dead husband's bed,
these hands murdered him.

If I must be exiled, never to see my family,
never to walk the soil of my country
so I will not sleep with my mother
and kill Polybos, my father, who raised me—his son!—
wasn't I born evil—answer me!—isn't every part of me
unclean? Oh
some unknown god, some savage venomous demon must   1070
    have done this,
raging, swollen with hatred. Hatred
for me.

Holiness, pure, radiant powers, o gods
don't let me see that day,
don't let it come, take me away
from men, men with their eyes, hide me
before I see
the filthy black stain reaching down over me, into me.

(*The* CHORUS *have moved away from the stage*)

LEADER Your words make us shudder, Oedipus,
        but hope, hope
        until you hear more from the man who witnessed the
            murder.

1080

OEDIPUS That is the only hope I have. Waiting.
         Waiting for that man to come from the pastures.

JOCASTA And when he finally comes, what do you hope to learn?

OEDIPUS If his story matches yours, I am saved.

JOCASTA What makes you say that?

OEDIPUS Bandits—you said he told you bandits killed Laios.
         So if he still talks about bandits,
         more than one, I couldn't have killed Laios.
         One man is not the same as many men.
         But if he speaks of one man, traveling alone,
         then all the evidence points to me.

1090

JOCASTA Believe me, Oedipus, those were his words.
         And he can't take them back: the whole city heard him,
             not only me.
         And if he changes only the smallest detail of his story,
         that still won't prove Laios was murdered as the oracle fore-
             told.
         Apollo was clear—it was Laios' fate to be killed by my son,

but my poor child died before his father died.
The future has no shape. The shapes of prophecy lie.
I see nothing in them, they are all illusions.   1100

OEDIPUS   Even so, I want that shepherd summoned here.
          Now. Do it now.

JOCASTA   I'll send for him immediately. But come inside.
          My only wish is to please you.

                                   JOCASTA *dispatches a servant.*

CHORUS   fate
          be here let what I say be pure
          let all my acts be pure
          laws forged in the huge clear fields of heaven
          rove the sky
          shaping my words limiting what I do   1110
          Olympos made those laws not men who live and die
          nothing lulls those laws to sleep
          they cannot die
          and the infinite god in them never ages

          arrogance insatiable pride
          breed the tyrant
          feed him on thing after thing blindly
          at the wrong time uselessly
          and he grows reaches so high   1120
          nothing can stop his fall
          his feet thrashing the air standing on nothing
          and nowhere to stand he plunges down
          o god shatter the tyrant
          but let men compete let self-perfection grow
          let men sharpen their skills
          soldiers citizens building the good city
          Apollo
          protect me always
          always the god I will honor   1130

62

if a man walks through his life arrogant
strutting proud
says anything does anything
does not fear justice
fear the gods bow to their shining presences
let fate make him stumble in his tracks
for all his lecheries and headlong greed
if he takes whatever he wants right or wrong
if he touches forbidden things
what man who acts like this would boast   1140
he can escape the anger of the gods
why should I join these sacred public dances
if such acts are honored

no
I will never go to the holy untouchable stone
navel of the earth at Delphi
never again
go to the temples at Olympia at Abai
if all these things are not joined
if past present future are not made one   1150
made clear to mortal eyes
o Zeus if that is your name
power above all immortal king
see these things look
those great prophecies are fading
men say they're nothing
nobody prays to the god of light no one believes
nothing of the gods stays

JOCASTA enters from the palace, carrying a branch tied with
strands of wool, and a jar of incense. She is accompanied by
                    a servant woman. She addresses the CHORUS.

JOCASTA Lords of Thebes, I come to the temples of the god
with offerings—this incense and this branch.   1160
So many thoughts torture Oedipus. He never rests.
He acts without reason. He is like a man

who has lost everything he knows—the past
is useless to him; strange, new things baffle him.
And if someone talks disaster, it stuns him: he listens, he is
        afraid.
I have tried to reassure him, but nothing helps.
So I have come to you—
Apollo, close to my life, close to this house,
listen to my prayers: (*she kneels*)
                                    help us purify ourselves of this disease,   1170
help us survive the long night of our suffering,
protect us. We are afraid when we see Oedipus confused
and frightened—Oedipus, the only man who can pilot
        Thebes
to safety.

A MESSENGER *from Corinth has arrived by the entrance to
the orchestra on the audience's left. He sees* JOCASTA *praying, then turns to address the* CHORUS.

MESSENGER Friends,
            can you tell me where King Oedipus lives
            or better still, where I can find him?

LEADER Here, in this house.
        This lady is his wife and mother
        of his children.   1180

MESSENGER May you and your family prosper.
            May you be happy always under this great roof.

JOCASTA Happiness and prosperity to you, too, for your kind words.
         But why are you here? Do you bring news?

MESSENGER Good news for your house, good news for King Oedipus.

JOCASTA What is your news? Who sent you?

MESSENGER I come from Corinth, and what I have to say I know will
                bring you joy.
            And pain perhaps. . . . I do not know.

JOCASTA Both joy and pain? What news could do that?

MESSENGER The people of Corinth want Oedipus as their king.   1190
That's what they're saying.

JOCASTA But isn't old Polybos still king of Corinth?

MESSENGER His kingdom is his grave.

JOCASTA Polybos is dead?

MESSENGER If I'm lying, my lady, let me die for it.

JOCASTA You. (*to a servant*) Go in and tell Oedipus.
O oracles of the gods, where are you now!
This man, the man Oedipus was afraid he would murder,
the man he feared, the man he fled from has died a natural
death.
Oedipus didn't kill him, it was luck, luck.   1200

She turns to greet OEDIPUS *as he comes out of the palace.*

OEDIPUS Jocasta, why did you send for me? (*taking her gently by the
arm*)

JOCASTA Oedipus,.
listen to this man, see what those ominous, holy predictions
of Apollo mean now.

OEDIPUS Who is this man? What does he say?

JOCASTA He comes from Corinth.
Your father is dead. Polybos is dead!

OEDIPUS What?
Let me hear those words from your own mouth, stranger.
Tell me yourself, in your own words.   1210

MESSENGER If that's what you want to hear first, then I'll say it:
Polybos is dead.

OEDIPUS How did he die? Assassination? Illness? How?

MESSENGER An old man's life hangs by a fragile thread. Anything can
         snap it.

OEDIPUS That poor old man. It was illness then?

MESSENGER Illness and old age.

OEDIPUS Why, Jocasta,
        why should men look to the great hearth at Delphi
        or listen to birds shrieking and wheeling overhead—
        cries meaning I was doomed to kill my father?   1220
        He is dead, gone, covered by the earth.
        And here I am—my hands never even touched a spear—
        I did not kill him,
        unless he died from wanting me to come home.
        No. Polybos has bundled up all these oracles
        and taken them with him to the world below.
        They are only words now, lost in the air.

JOCASTA Isn't that what I predicted?

OEDIPUS You were right. My fears confused me.

JOCASTA You have nothing to fear. Not now. Not ever.   1230

OEDIPUS But the oracle said I am doomed to sleep with my mother.
        How can I live with that and not be afraid?

JOCASTA Why should men be afraid of anything? Fortune rules our
        lives.
        Luck is everything. Things happen. The future is darkness.
        No human mind can know it.
        It's best to live in the moment, live for today, Oedipus.
        Why should the thought of marrying your mother make
        you so afraid?
        Many men have slept with their mothers in their dreams.

Why worry? See your dreams for what they are—nothing,
   nothing at all.
Be happy, Oedipus.   1240

OEDIPUS   All that you say is right, Jocasta. I know it.
I should be happy,
but my mother is still living. As long as she's alive,
I live in fear. This fear is necessary.
I have no choice.

JOCASTA   But Oedipus, your father's death is a sign, a great sign—
the sky has cleared, the sun's gaze holds us in its warm,
   hopeful light.

OEDIPUS   A great sign, I agree. But so long as my mother is alive,
my fear lives too.

MESSENGER   Who is this woman you fear so much?   1250

OEDIPUS   Merope, King Polybos' wife.

MESSENGER   Why does Merope frighten you so much?

OEDIPUS   A harrowing oracle hurled down upon us by some great god.

MESSENGER   Can you tell me? Or did the god seal your lips?

OEDIPUS   I can.
Long ago, Apollo told me I was doomed to sleep with my
   mother
and spill my father's blood, murder him
with these two hands of mine.
That's why I never returned to Corinth. Luckily, it would
   seem.
Still, nothing on earth is sweeter to a man's eyes   1260
than the sight of his father and mother.

MESSENGER   And you left Corinth because of this prophecy?

OEDIPUS Yes. And because of my father. To avoid killing my father.

MESSENGER But didn't my news prove you have nothing to fear?
I brought good news.

OEDIPUS And I will reward you for your kindness.

MESSENGER That's why I came, my lord. I knew you'd remember me
when you returned to Corinth.

OEDIPUS I will never return, never live with my parents again.

MESSENGER Son, it's clear you don't know what you're doing.   1270

OEDIPUS What do you mean? In the name of the gods, speak.

MESSENGER If you're afraid to go home because of your parents.

OEDIPUS I am afraid, afraid
Apollo's prediction will come true, all of it,
as god's sunlight grows brighter on a man's face at dawn
when he's in bed, still sleeping,
and reaches into his eyes and wakes him.

MESSENGER Afraid of murdering your father, of having his blood
on your hands?

OEDIPUS Yes. His blood. The stain of his blood. That terror never   1280
leaves me.

MESSENGER But Oedipus, then you have no reason to be afraid.

OEDIPUS I'm their son, they're my parents, aren't they?

MESSENGER Polybos is nothing to you.

OEDIPUS Polybos is not my father?

MESSENGER No more than I am.

OEDIPUS But you are nothing to me. Nothing.

MESSENGER And Polybos is nothing to you either.

OEDIPUS Then why did he call me his son?

MESSENGER Because I gave you to him. With these hands
I gave you to him.   1290

OEDIPUS How could he have loved me like a father if I am not his son?

MESSENGER He had no children. That opened his heart.

OEDIPUS And what about you?
Did you buy me from someone? Or did you find me?

MESSENGER I found you squawling, left alone to die in the thickets of
Kithairon.

OEDIPUS Kithairon? What were you doing on Kithairon?

MESSENGER Herding sheep in the high summer pastures.

OEDIPUS You were a shepherd, a drifter looking for work?

MESSENGER A drifter, yes, but it was I who saved you.

OEDIPUS Saved me? Was I hurt when you picked me up?   1300

MESSENGER Ask your feet.

OEDIPUS Why,
why did you bring up that childhood pain?

MESSENGER I cut you free. Your feet were pierced, tied together at the ankles
with leather thongs strung between the tendons and the bone.

OEDIPUS That mark of my shame—I've worn it from the cradle.

MESSENGER   That mark is the meaning of your name:
             Oedipus, Swollenfoot, Oedipus.

OEDIPUS   Oh gods
             who did this to me?   1310
             My mother?
             My father?

MESSENGER   I don't know. The man I took you from—he would know.

OEDIPUS   So you didn't find me? Somebody else gave me to you?

MESSENGER   I got you from another shepherd.

OEDIPUS   What shepherd? Who was he? Do you know?

MESSENGER   As I recall, he worked for Laios.

OEDIPUS   The same Laios who was king of Thebes?

MESSENGER   The same Laios. The man was one of Laios' shepherds.

OEDIPUS   Is he still alive? I want to see this man.   1320

MESSENGER   (pointing to the CHORUS) These people would know that better
                 than I do.

OEDIPUS   Do any of you know this shepherd he's talking about?
             Have you ever noticed him in the fields or in the city?
             Answer, if you have.
             It is time everything came out, time everything was made clear.
             Everything.

LEADER   I think he's the shepherd you sent for.
             But Jocasta, she would know.

OEDIPUS   (to JOCASTA)
             Jocasta, do you know this man?
             Is he the man this shepherd here says worked for Laios?   1330

JOCASTA What man? Forget about him. Forget what was said.
         It's not worth talking about.

OEDIPUS How can I forget
         with clues like these in my hands?
         With the secret of my birth staring me in the face?

JOCASTA No, Oedipus!
         No more questions.
         For god's sake, for the sake of your own life!
         Isn't my anguish enough—more than enough?

OEDIPUS You have nothing to fear, Jocasta.   1340
         Even if my mother
         and her mother before her were both slaves,
         that doesn't make you the daughter of slaves.

JOCASTA Oedipus, you must stop.
                                   I beg you—stop!

OEDIPUS Nothing can stop me now. I must know everything.
         Everything!

JOCASTA I implore you, Oedipus. For your own good.

OEDIPUS Damn my own good!

JOCASTA Oh, Oedipus, Oedipus,   1350
         I pray to god you never see who you are!

OEDIPUS (to one of the attendants, who hurries off through the
               exit stage left)
         You there, go find that shepherd, bring him here.
         Let that woman bask in the glory of her noble birth.

JOCASTA God help you, Oedipus—
         you were born to suffer, born
         to misery and grief.

These are the last last words I will ever speak, ever
Oedipus.

(JOCASTA *rushes offstage into the palace. Long silence.*)

LEADER Why did Jocasta rush away,
Oedipus, fleeing in such pain?   1360
I fear disaster, or worse,
will break from this silence of hers.

OEDIPUS Let it break! Let everything break!
I must discover who I am, know the secret of my birth,
no matter how humble, how vile.
Perhaps Jocasta is ashamed of my low birth, ashamed to be my
       wife.
Like all women she's proud.
But Luck, goddess who gives men all that is good, made me,
and I won't be cheated of what is mine, nothing can dishonor
       me, ever.
I am like the months, my brothers the months—they   1370
       shaped me
when I was a baby in the cold hills of Kithairon,
they guided me, carved out my times of greatness,
and they still move their hands over my life.
I am the man I am. I will not stop
until I discover who my parents are.

CHORUS if I know if I see
if the dark force of prophecy is mine
Kithairon
when the full moon
rides over us tomorrow   1380
listen listen to us sing to you
dance worship praise you
mountain where Oedipus was found
know Oedipus will praise you
praise his nurse country and mother
who blessed our king

I call on you Apollo
let these visions please you
god Apollo
healer   1390

Oedipus son
who was your mother
which of the deathless mountain nymphs who lay
with the great god Pan
on the high peaks he runs across
or with Apollo
who loves the high green pastures above
which one bore you
did the god of the bare windy peaks Hermes
or the wild, dervish Dionysos   1400
living in the cool air of the hills
take you
a foundling
from one of the nymphs he plays with
joyously lift you hold you in his arms

OEDIPUS Old men, I think the man coming toward us now
    must be the shepherd we are looking for.
    I have never seen him, but the years, chalking his face and
        hair, tell me
    he's the man. And my men are with him. But you probably
        know him.

LEADER I do know him. If Laios ever had a man he trusted,   1410
    this was the man.

OEDIPUS (to the MESSENGER)
    You—is this the man you told me about?

MESSENGER That's him. You're looking at the man.

OEDIPUS (to the SHEPHERD who has been waiting, hanging back)
    You there, come closer.

                              Answer me, old man.
          Did you work for Laios?

SHEPHERD I was born his slave, and grew up in his household.

OEDIPUS What was your work?

SHEPHERD Herding sheep, all my life.

OEDIPUS Where?   1420

SHEPHERD Kithairon, mostly. And the country around Kithairon.

OEDIPUS Do you remember ever seeing this man?

MESSENGER Which man?

OEDIPUS (pointing to the MESSENGER)
          This man standing here. Have you ever seen him before?

SHEPHERD Not that I remember.

MESSENGER No wonder, master. But I'll make him remember.
          He knows who I am. We used to graze our flocks together
          in the pastures around Kithairon.
          Every year, for six whole months, three years running.
          From March until September, when the Dipper rose, signaling 1430
               the harvest.
          I had one flock, he had two.
          And when the frost came, I drove my sheep back to their
               winter pens
          and he drove his back to Laios' fold.
          Remember, old man? Isn't that how it was?

SHEPHERD Yes. But it was all so long ago.

MESSENGER And do you remember giving me a baby boy at the time—
          to raise as my own son?

SHEPHERD What if I do? Why all these questions?

MESSENGER That boy became King Oedipus, friend.

SHEPHERD Damn you, can't you keep quiet.   1440

OEDIPUS Don't scold him, old man.
It's you who deserve to be punished, not him.

SHEPHERD What did I say, good master?

OEDIPUS You haven't answered his question about the boy.

SHEPHERD He's making trouble, master. He doesn't know a thing.

(OEDIPUS *takes the* SHEPHERD *by the cloak*)

OEDIPUS Tell me or you'll be sorry.

SHEPHERD For god's sake, don't hurt me, I'm an old man.

OEDIPUS (*to one of his men*) You there, hold him. We'll make him
talk.

(*The attendant pins the* SHEPHERD'*s arms behind his back*)

SHEPHERD Oedipus, Oedipus,
god knows I pity you.
What more do you want to know?   1450

OEDIPUS Did you give the child to this man?
Speak.   Yes or no?

SHEPHERD Yes.
And I wish to god I'd died that day.

OEDIPUS You *will* be dead unless you tell me the whole truth.

SHEPHERD And worse than dead, if I do.

OEDIPUS It seems our man won't answer.

SHEPHERD No. I told you already. I gave him the boy.

OEDIPUS Where did you get him? From Laios' household? Or where?

SHEPHERD He wasn't my child. He was given to me.   1460

OEDIPUS (turning to the CHORUS and the audience)
         By whom? Someone here in Thebes?

SHEPHERD Master, please, in god's name, no more questions.

OEDIPUS You're a dead man if I have to ask you once more.

SHEPHERD He was one
          of the children
          from Laios'
          household.

OEDIPUS A slave child? Or Laios' own?

SHEPHERD I can't say it . . . it's
          awful, the words   1470
          are awful . . . awful.

OEDIPUS And I,
         I am afraid to hear them . . .
         but I must.

SHEPHERD He was Laios' own child.
          Your wife, inside the palace, she can explain it all.

OEDIPUS She gave you the child?

SHEPHERD My lord . . . yes.

OEDIPUS Why?

SHEPHERD She wanted me to abandon the child on a mountain.   1480

OEDIPUS His own mother?

SHEPHERD Yes. There were prophecies, horrible oracles. She was afraid.

OEDIPUS What oracles?

SHEPHERD Oracles predicting he would murder his own father.

OEDIPUS But why did you give the boy to this old man?

SHEPHERD Because I pitied him, master, because I
thought the man would take the child away, take him to another
    country.
Instead he saved him. Saved him for—oh gods,
a fate so horrible, so awful, words can't describe it.
If you were the baby that man took from me, Oedipus,   1490
what misery, what grief is yours!

OEDIPUS (*looking up at the sun*)
LIGHT   LIGHT   LIGHT
never again flood these eyes with your white radiance, oh
    gods, my eyes. All, all
the oracles have proven true. I, Oedipus, I
am the child
of parents who should never have been mine—doomed,
    doomed!
Now everything is clear—I
lived with a woman, she was my mother, I slept in my
    mother's bed, and I
murdered, murdered my father,
the man whose blood flows in these veins of mine,   1500
whose blood stains these two hands red.

OEDIPUS *raises his hands to the sun, then turns and walks into*
                                                    the palace.

77

CHORUS man after man after man
o mortal generations
here once
almost not here
what are we
dust ghosts images a rustling of air
nothing nothing
we breathe on the abyss
we are the abyss   1510
our happiness no more than traces of a dream
the high noon sun sinking into the sea
the red spume of its wake raining behind it
we are you
we are you Oedipus
dragging your maimed foot
in agony
and now that I see your life finally revealed
your life fused with the god
blazing out of the black nothingness of all we know   1520
I say
no happiness lasts nothing human lasts

wherever you aimed you hit
no archer had your skill
you grew rich powerful great
everything came falling to your feet
o Zeus
after he killed the Sphinx
whose claws curled under
whose weird song of the future baffled and destroyed   1530
he stood like a tower high above our country
warding off death
and from then on Oedipus we called you
king our king
draped you in gold
our highest honors were yours
and you ruled this shining city
Thebes   Thebes

now
your story is pain pity no story is worse   1540
than yours Oedipus
ruined savage blind
as you struggle with your life
as your life changes
and breaks and shows you who you are
Oedipus   Oedipus
son father you harbored in the selfsame place
the same place sheltered you both
bridegroom
how could the furrow your father plowed   1550
not have cried out all this time
while you lay there unknowing
and saw the truth too late

time like the sun sees all things
and it sees you
you cannot hide from that light
your own life opening itself to you
to all
married unmarried father son
for so long   1560
justice comes like the dawn
always
and it shows the world your marriage now

I wish
o child of Laios
I wish I had never seen you
I grieve for you
wail after wail fills me and pours out
because of you my breath came flowing back
but now   1570
the darkness of your life
floods my eyes

The palace doors open. A SERVANT *enters and approaches the*
                                    CHORUS *and audience.*

SERVANT Noble citizens, honored above all others in Thebes,
     if you still care for the house of Laios,
     if you still can feel the spirit of those who ruled before, now
     the horrors you will hear, the horrors you will see, will shake
        your hearts and shatter you with grief beyond enduring.
     Not even the waters of those great rivers Ister and Phasis
     could wash away the blood
     that now darkens every stone of this shining house,   1580
     this house that will reveal, soon, soon
     the misery and evil two mortals,
     both masters of this house, have brought upon themselves.

     The griefs we cause ourselves cut deepest of all.

LEADER What we already know
     has hurt us enough,
     has made us cry out in pain.
     What more can you say?

SERVANT This:
     Jocasta is dead. The queen is dead.   1590

LEADER Ah, poor
     unhappy Jocasta,
     how did she die?

SERVANT She killed herself. She did it.
     But you did not see what happened there,
     you were not there, in the palace. You did not see it.
     I did.
     I will tell you how Queen Jocasta died,
     the whole story, all of it. All I can remember.
     After her last words to Oedipus   1600
     she rushed past us through the entrance hall, screaming,
     raking her hair with both hands, and flew into the bedroom,
        their bedroom,
     and slammed the doors shut as she lunged at her bridal bed,
     crying "Laios" "Laios"—dead all these years—

remembering Laios—how his own son years ago
grew up and then killed him, leaving her to
sleep with her own son, to have his children, *their* children,
children—not sons, not daughters, something else, mon-
        sters. . . .
Then she collapsed, sobbing, cursing the bed where she held
        both men in her arms,
got husband from husband, children from her child.   1610
We heard it all, but suddenly, I couldn't tell what was hap-
        pening.
Oedipus came crashing in, he was howling,
stalking up and down—we couldn't take our eyes off him—
and we stopped listening to her pitiful cries.
We stood there, watching him move like a bull, lurching,
        charging,
shouting at each of us to give him a sword, demanding we
        tell him
where his wife was, that woman whose womb carried him,
him and his children, that wife who gave him birth.
Some god, some demon, led him to her, and he knew—
none of us showed him—   1620
suddenly a mad, inhuman cry burst from his mouth
as if the wind rushed through his tortured body,
and he heaved against those bedroom doors so the hinges
        whined
and bent from their sockets and the bolts snapped,
and he stood in the room.
There she was—
we could see her—his wife
dangling by her neck from a noose of braided, silken cords
tied to a rafter, still swaying.
And when he saw her he bellowed and stretched up and   1630
        loosened the rope,
cradling her in one arm,
and slowly laid her body on the ground.

That's when it happened—he
ripped off the gold

brooches she was wearing—one on each shoulder of her
        gown—
and raised them over his head—you could see them flashing—
and tilted his face up and
brought them right down into his eyes
and the long pins sank deep, all the way back into the sockets,
and he shouted at his eyes: 1640
"Now you won't see me, you won't see
my agonies or my crimes,
but in endless darkness, always, there you'll see
those I never should have seen.
And those I should have known were my parents, father and
        mother—
these eyes will never see their faces in the light.
These eyes will never see the light again, never."
Cursing his two blind eyes over and over, he
lifted the brooches again and drove their pins through his
        eyeballs up
to the hilts until they were pulp, until the blood streamed out   1650
soaking his beard and cheeks,
a black storm splashing its hail across his face.

Two mortals acted. Now grief tears their lives apart
as if that pain sprang from a single, sorrowing root
to curse each one, man and wife. For all those years
their happiness was truly happiness, but now, now
wailing, madness, shame and death,
every evil men have given a name,
everything criminal and vile
that mankind suffers they suffer. Not one evil is missing.   1660

LEADER But now
        does this torn, anguished man
        have any rest from his pain?

SERVANT No, no—
        then he shouted at us to open the doors and show everyone
                in Thebes

82

his father's killer, his mother's—I cannot say it.
Once we have seen him as he is
he will leave Thebes, lift the curse from his city—
banish himself, cursed by his own curses.
But his strength is gone, his whole life is pain,   1670
more pain than any man can bear.
He needs help, someone to guide him.
He is alone, and blind. Look,
look—the palace doors are opening—now
a thing
so horrible will stand before you
you will shudder with disgust and try to turn away
while your hearts will swell with pity for what you see.

The central doors open. OEDIPUS *enters, led by his household*
servants. His mask is covered with blood. The CHORUS *begin a*
dirge to which OEDIPUS *responds antiphonally.*

CHORUS   horror horror o what suffering
              men see   1680
              but none is worse than this
              Oedipus o
              how could you have slashed out your eyes
              what god leaped on you
              from beyond the last border of space
              what madness entered you
              clawing even more misery into you
              I cannot look at you

              but there are questions
              so much I would know   1690
              so much that I would see
              no   no
              the shape of your life makes me shudder

OEDIPUS   I   I
              this voice of agony
              I am   what place am I
              where? Not here, nowhere I know!

What force, what tide breaks over my life?
Pain, demon stabbing into me
leaving nothing, nothing, no man I know, not human,   1700
fate howling out of nowhere   what am I
fire   a voice   where   where
is it being taken?

LEADER   Beyond everything to a place
so terrible nothing is seen there, nothing is heard.

OEDIPUS   (*reaching out, groping*)
Thing   thing   darkness
spilling into me, my
black cloud smothering me forever,
nothing can stop you, nothing can escape,
I cannot push you away.   1710

I am
nothing but my own cries breaking
again and again
the agony of those gold pins
the memory of what I did
stab me
again
again.

LEADER   What can you feel but pain.
It all comes back, pain in remorse,   1720
remorse in pain, to tear you apart with grief.

OEDIPUS   Dear, loyal friend
you, only you, are still here with me, still care
for this blind, tortured man.
Oh,
I know you are there, I know you, friend,
even in this darkness, friend, touched by your voice.

LEADER   What you did was horrible,

but how could you quench the fire of your eyes,
what demon lifted your hands?   1730

OEDIPUS Apollo   Apollo
          it was Apollo, always Apollo,
          who brought each of my agonies to birth,
          but I,
          nobody else, I,
          I raised these two hands of mine, held them above my head,
          and plunged them down,
          I stabbed out these eyes.
          Why should I have eyes? Why,
          when nothing I saw was worth seeing?   1740
          Nothing.

LEADER Nothing. Nothing.

OEDIPUS Oh friends. Nothing.
          No one to see, no one to love,
          no one to speak to, no one to hear!
                    Friends, friends, lead me away now.
          Lead me away from Thebes—Oedipus,
          destroyer and destroyed,
          the man whose life is hell
          for others and for himself, the man   1750
          more hated by the gods than any other man, ever.

LEADER Oh I pity you,
          I weep for your fate
          and for your mind,
          for what it is to be you, Oedipus.
          I wish you had never seen the man you are.

OEDIPUS I hate
          the man who found me, cut the thongs from my feet,
          snatched me from death, cared for me—
          I wish he were dead!   1760

I should have died up there on those wild, desolate slopes of
    Kithairon.
Then my pain and the pain
those I love suffer now
never would have been.

LEADER These are my wishes too.

OEDIPUS Then I never would have murdered my father,
never heard men call me my mother's husband.

Now
I am
Oedipus!   1770
Oedipus, who lay in that loathsome bed, made love there in
    that bed,
his father's and mother's bed, the bed
where he was born.

No gods anywhere now, not for me, now,
unholy, broken man.
What man ever suffered grief like this?

LEADER How can I say that what you did was right?
Better to be dead than live blind.

OEDIPUS I did what I had to do. No more advice.
How could my eyes,   1780
when I went down into that black, sightless place beneath
    the earth,
the place where the dead go down, how,
how could I have looked at anything,
with what human eyes could I have gazed
on my father, on my mother—
oh gods, my mother!
What I did against those two
not even strangling could punish.

And my children, how would the sight of them, born as
    they were born,
be sweet? Not to these eyes of mine, never to these eyes.   1790
Nothing, nothing is left me now—no city with its high walls,
no shining statues of the gods. I stripped all these things
    from myself—
I, Oedipus, fallen lower than any man now, born nobler
    than the best,
born the king of Thebes! Cursed with my own curses, I
commanded Thebes to drive out the killer.
I banished the royal son of Laios, the man the gods revealed
is stained with the awful stain. The secret stain
that I myself revealed is my stain. And now, revealed at last,
how could I ever look men in the eyes?
Never. Never.   1800

If I could, I would have walled my ears so they heard nothing,
I would have made this body of mine a wall.
I would have heard nothing, tasted nothing, smelled noth-
    ing, seen
nothing.
            No thought. No feeling. Nothing. Nothing.
So pain would never reach me any more.

O Kithairon,
why did you shelter me and take me in?
Why did you let me live? Better to have died on that bare
    slope of yours
where no man would ever have seen me or known the secret   1810
    of my birth!

Polybos, Corinth, that house I thought was my father's home,
how beautiful I was when you sheltered me as a child
and oh what disease festered beneath that beauty.
Now everyone knows the secret of my birth, knows
how vile I am.

O roads, secret valley, cluster of oaks,

O narrow place where two roads join a third,
roads that drank my blood as it streamed from my hands,
flowing from my dead father's body,
do you remember me now?   1820
Do you remember what I did with my own two hands, there
        in your presence,
and what I did after that, when I came here to Thebes?
O marriage, marriage, you gave me my life, and then
from the same seed, my seed, spewed out
fathers, brothers, sisters, children, brides, wives—
nothing, no words can express the shame.
No more words. Men should not name what men should
        never do.

                                    (*To the* CHORUS)

Gods, oh gods, gods,
hide me, hide me
now   1830
far away from Thebes,
kill me,
cast me into the sea,
drive me where you will never see me—never again.

                    (*Reaching out to the* CHORUS, *who back away*)

Touch this poor man, touch me,
don't be afraid to touch me. Believe me, nobody,
nobody but me can bear
this fire of anguish.
It is mine. Mine.

LEADER Kreon has come.   1840
        Now he, not you, is the sole guardian of Thebes,
        and only he can grant you what you ask.

OEDIPUS (*turning toward the palace*)
        What can I say to him, how can anything I say

make him listen now?
I wronged him. I accused him, and now everything I said
proves I am vile.

KREON (*enters from the entrance to the right. He is accompanied
            by men who gather around* OEDIPUS)

I have not come to mock you, Oedipus; I have not come to
    blame you for the past.

(*To attendánts*)

You men, standing there, if you have no respect for human
        dignity,
at least revere the master of life,
the all-seeing sun whose light nourishes   1850
every living thing on earth.
Come, cover this cursed, naked, holy thing, hide him
from the earth and the sacred rain and the light,
you powers who cringe from his touch.
Take him. Do it now. Be reverent.
Only his family should see and hear his grief.
Their grief.

OEDIPUS I beg you, Kreon, if you love the gods,
    grant me what I ask.
I have been vile to you, worse than vile.   1860
I have hurt you, terribly, and yet
you have treated me with kindness, with nobility.
You have calmed my fear, you did not turn away from me.
Do what I ask. Do it for yourself, not for me.

KREON What do you want from me, Oedipus?

OEDIPUS Drive me out of Thebes, do it now, now—
    drive me someplace where no man can speak to me,
    where no man can see me anymore.

KREON Believe me, Oedipus, I would have done it long ago.
But I refuse to act until I know precisely what the god de-   1870
sires.

OEDIPUS Apollo has revealed what he desires. Everything is clear.
I killed my father, I am polluted and unclean.
I must die.

KREON That is what the god commanded, Oedipus.
But there are no precedents for what has happened.
We need to *know* before we act.

OEDIPUS Do you care so much for me, enough to ask Apollo?
For *me*, Oedipus?

KREON Now even you will trust the god, I think.

OEDIPUS I will. And I turn to you, I implore you, Kreon—   1880
the woman lying dead inside, your sister,
give her whatever burial you think best.
                                        As for me,
never let this city of my fathers see me here in Thebes.
Let me go and live on the mountain, on Kithairon—the
    mountain
my parents intended for my grave.
Let me die the way they wanted me to die: slowly, alone—
die *their* way.
And yet this much I know—
                                no sickness,   1890
no ordinary, natural death is mine.
I have been saved, preserved, kept alive
for some strange fate, for something far more awful still.
When that thing comes, let it take me
where it will.

(OEDIPUS *turns, looking for something, waiting*)

As for my sons, Kreon,
they are grown men, they can look out for themselves.

But my daughters, those two poor girls of mine,
who have never left their home before, never left their
     father's side,
who ate at my side every day, who shared whatever was   1900
     mine,
I beg you, Kreon,
care for them, love them.
But more than anything, Kreon,
I want to touch them,

                              (*he begins to lift his hands*)

let me touch them with these hands of mine,
let them come to me so we can grieve together.
My noble lord, if only I could touch them with my hands,
they would still be mine just as they were
when I had eyes that could still see.

(*Oedipus' two small daughters are brought out of the palace*)

O gods, gods, is it possible? Do I hear   1910
my two daughters crying? Has Kreon pitied me and brought
     me
what I love more than my life—
my daughters?

KREON I brought them to you, knowing how much you love them,
             Oedipus,
        knowing the joy you would feel if they were here.

OEDIPUS May the gods who watch over the path of your life, Kreon,
            prove kinder to you than they were to me.
            Where are you, children?
            Come, come to your brother's hands—

            (*taking his daughters into his arms*)

            his mother was your mother, too,   1920

come to these hands which made these eyes, bright clear eyes
    once,
sockets seeing nothing, the eyes
of the man who fathered you. Look . . . your father's eyes,
your father—
who knew nothing until now, saw nothing until now, and
    became
the husband of the woman who gave him birth.

                                        I weep for you
when I think how men will treat you, how bitter your lives
    will be.
What festivals will you attend, whose homes will you visit
and not be assailed by whispers, and people's stares?   1930
Where will you go and not leave in tears?
And when the time comes for you to marry,
what men will take you as their brides, and risk the shame of
    marrying
the daughters of Oedipus?
What sorrow will not be yours?
Your father killed his father, made love
to the woman who gave birth to him. And he fathered you
in the same place where he was fathered.
That is what you will hear; that is what they will say.
Who will marry you then? You will never marry,   1940
but grow hard and dry like wheat so far beyond harvest
that the wind blows its white flakes into the winter sky.
Oh Kreon,
now you are the only father my daughters have.
Jocasta and I, their parents, are lost to them forever.
These poor girls are yours. Your blood.
Don't let them wander all their lives.
begging, alone, unmarried, helpless.
Don't let them suffer as their father has. Pity them, Kreon,
pity these girls, so young and helpless except for you.   1950
Promise me this. Noble Kreon,
touch me with your hand, give me a sign.

                                  (KREON takes his hands)

Daughters,
daughters, if you were older, if you could understand,
there is so much more I would say to you.
But for now, I give you this prayer—

Live,
live your lives, live each day as best you can,
may your lives be happier than your father's was.

KREON No more grief Come in.   1960

OEDIPUS I must. But obedience comes hard.

KREON Everything has its time.

OEDIPUS First, promise me this.

KREON Name it.

OEDIPUS Banish me from Thebes.

KREON I cannot.   Ask the gods for that.

OEDIPUS The gods hate me.

KREON Then you will have your wish.

OEDIPUS You promise?

KREON I say only what I mean.   1970

OEDIPUS Then lead me in.

      (OEDIPUS *reaches out and touches his daughters, trying to*
take them with him)

KREON Oedipus, come with me. Let your daughters go. Come.

OEDIPUS No. You will not take my daughters. I forbid it.

KREON You *forbid* me?
       You have no power any more.
       All the great power you once had is gone,
       gone forever.

The CHORUS *turn to face the audience.* KREON *leads* OEDIPUS
toward the palace. His daughters follow. He moves slowly,
                and disappears into the palace as the CHORUS *ends.*

CHORUS O citizens of Thebes, this is Oedipus,
        who solved the famous riddle, who held more power
               than any mortal.
        See what he is: all men gazed on his fortunate life,   1980
        all men envied him, but look at him, look.
        All he had, all this man was,
        pulled down and swallowed by the storm of his own life,
        and by the god.
        Keep your eyes on that last day, on your dying.
        Happiness and peace, they were not yours
        unless at death you can look back on your life and say
        I lived, I did not suffer.

PRELIMINARY NOTE

Formally, the Oedipus has the articulations of every Greek tragedy. It is built out of a Prologue, or opening scene, a Parodos, or the entrance song of the Chorus, and song and speech alternate throughout the play. What follows the Parodos is the first of four "episodes" which alternate with stasima, or sections of choral song. The last episode was called the Exodos, or exit scene. Aristotle distinguished between the Parodos and stasima (Poetics 12.1452b22), but the most fundamental distinction between the "parts" of a Greek tragedy is between song and speech, dance and the stage. Like the choral songs, the Parodos was sung or chanted in a dialect and in rhythms that were distinct from the Attic dialect and mainly iambic rhythm of the spoken parts. Thus, the Prologue, episodes, and exodos are the spoken parts of the play. The sung or lyrical parts of the Oedipus are made up of the entrance song of the Chorus, four choral songs (stasima), and two kommoi, or dirges sung in an antiphonal recitative between Oedipus on stage and the Chorus in the orchestra (853-912, 1679-1776). The stasimon which follows Jocasta's discovery of the truth about her son and marriage is part of an excited dance form known as a hypórchema (1376-1405). Formally, and fundamentally, the middle of Oedipus is the song beginning "Fate be here let what I say be pure."

The lyrical parts of the Oedipus have a movement, language, rhythm, and logic of their own. Our manuscripts of the Greek text of Sophocles do not record the music that accompanied the choral song. They do not give us a choreography for how the dancers moved in the orchestra, and they give us only clues to what the audience in the theater of Dionysos saw before them. Fifteen dancers (choreutai) moved onto the dancing floor just below the low stage platform, led by a flute-player. They move, sing together in a rectangular formation of five rows (facing the audience), three deep. At the center of the first row is the "head man" or Leader of the Chorus—the Koryphaios. The Chorus sing in unison, and speak, and are spoken to, as one man. The Chorus of the *Oedipus* are made up of Theban elders, summoned to the palace (and stage) by Oedipus who asked the people of Kadmos to assemble before his palace.

The particles and logic which control the thought and emotion of the language of the actors on stage do not carry over into the Chorus. In Greek dramatic lyric, as in the choral songs of Pindar and Bacchylides, verbs are rare and they control, with inevitable and deliberate ambiguities, large stretches of the song they inform. Because of a lyrical lack of subordination in the logic of the Chorus' song, the audience, who are closer to the Chorus than they are to the actors onstage, are compelled to become a part of the Chorus and to supply themselves the necessary and subtle ligatures that bind phrase to phrase. And as in the language of Greek cultic poetry, compound epithets are nets with which men attempt to snare and contain the power of their gods. Thought moves from *strophe* to *antistrophe*: turn and return. In the first movement of their entrance song, the Chorus invoke the voice of prophecy; in the *antistrophe*, they call upon Athena. Apollo occupies the same place in both *strophe* and *antistrophe*. We have attempted to reproduce in English, which has no tradition for this kind of song, the essential gaps and ambiguities of Greek choral song by a kind of Broken Poetry. We have also attempted to capture and reproduce the overarching thematic unities that make a whole of this Broken Poetry.

A part of the ancient lore which fills the margins of our manuscripts of Aristophanes' *Frogs* is an explanation and derivation of the word *stasimon*: "this is the part the dancers sing when they are stationary." What this means is not that the Chorus are rooted to the dancing floor; they are not. Rather they have taken their positions on the dancing floor. The action of the *Oedipus* does not come to a standstill with the sections of lyrical song. What has been said and done on stage moves onto another plane of reaction and reflection, which often mirrors the action of the play as a whole rather than the facets of its development. Formal and conservative, in the sense that old men are conservative and wed to traditional values, and fundamentally *polis*-bound, the Chorus are physically and naturally the intermediaries between the audience and the remote hero who moves above them on the tragic stage.

Sophocles' Chorus was fifteen in number, his actors three. There were also a number of silent actors on stage. All Greek tragedies were contests (*agones*), and the actors in these contests were called *agonistai*. The most important of these, the Protagonist, played the part of Oedipus. There is no difficulty in assigning the parts taken by the second and third actors. It is sure that Sophocles would have given the same actor the parts of Teiresias and the old shepherd who saved Oedipus' life.

NOTES ON THE TEXT

1-182 Prologue

3 *those branches tied with wool*   A delegation of Thebans has come to the palace
of Oedipus and taken up the position of suppliants before the stage
and the altar of Apollo. They have placed branches twined with wool
on the altar as an offering to Apollo, the god whose oracles shape the
plot of the *Oedipus* and who was also a god of healing. In the *Iliad*,
Apollo was the god of plague.

21 In his description of the three ages of the suppliants who have gathered before
the palace of Thebes, the priest seems to give a faint hint of the human condition and the riddle of the Sphinx; cf. the note to 156.

22 *around your altar*   Immediately, the altar that belongs to the stage and the
palace of Thebes. But the ambiguity of Sophocles' language takes in
Oedipus in its suggestion that Oedipus is a god (cf. 58, and 50, where
the suggestion is denied). Thebes calls Oedipus *soter*, saviour, and
Oedipus appears (at 286) in response to the prayers of the Chorus
(cf. 244).

26 *the two great temples of Athena*   One of these must have been the temple of
Athena Ongka. It is not clear which aspect of the goddess the second
temple honored, but in Athens there were two temples to Athena on
the Acropolis. These temples and the plague are two of the bonds
uniting Thebes and Athens in the *Oedipus*. Cf. Introduction v and
the note to 1978.

27 *staring into the ashes* At the oracular shrine of Apollo Ismenios, where the behavior of things such as incense or flour placed in the fire of the altar declared symbolically the configuration of the past, present, or future. His altar was made of ash, and he was called Ashen Apollo.

63 *our plans and their results* In Greek the outcome of the plans of men of experience is called *symphoras*—a word that usually means disaster. It describes the plague in 121 and Oedipus' fate in 1983. Here this (disastrous) outcome is said to *live*—like the oracles that wheel around the head of the doomed man in 659.

92 *great Apollo's shrine at Delphi* To the temple of Apollo at Delphi where the god and his priestess, the Pythia, gave oracles revealing not only the future, but the hidden past and present. At the entrance to the temple was an inscription which read: "Know thyself," GNOTHI SAUTON.

115 *Cleanse the city of Thebes* The Greek word is *miasma*—pollution. What this pollution comes from is the stain of his father's blood on Oedipus' hands. For the Greek, *miasma* was something palpable and contagious. The verb "to pollute," "defile," also means to stain. The connection between these two notions is strikingly apparent in the Homeric simile which likens the blood spreading over the wounded Menelaos' thighs to the dye with which a woman stains ivory (*Iliad* 4.141-147). In Homer's Greek the word for the staining of dye and the staining of blood is the same (*miainein*). The product of staining is *miasma*. Oedipus uses a similar word (*kelis*) for his own defilement: "the filthy black stain reaching down over me" (1078); his hands bloody the bed of the man he killed (1062). Oedipus is unclean, and Apollo gives Thebes a choice of purifications: either fresh blood is needed to wash away the blood of the murdered man, or the source of taint and disease (*miasma*) must be driven from Thebes. Apollo's language—"you must drive the man out"—suggests the religious term for driving an *agos*, or source of defilement, from a city (cf. 543). In the course of the *Oedipus*, the doomed man of Apollo's prophecy becomes an *agos*—a thing both sacred and cursed (see the note to 1852).

There is still another word for this pollution in the *Oedipus*—*mysos*, "this stain, this disease" (167); Oedipus pronounces it, and it is known in Sophocles only here. *Mysos* is a word with distinct and significant associations: in Aeschylus it described the defilement of a woman who had murdered her husband and a son who had shed his mother's blood (*Choephoroi*, 650; *Eumenides*, 838; cf. Empedocles, *Purifications*, fragments 137 and 115, translated in the note to 1852). Here, in a discord between the appearances of the play and the hidden realities known to Sophocles' audience, we confront one of the most subtle ironies of the *Oedipus*. Appearance is that the source of the pollution and plague that infest Thebes is the blood on the hands of an unknown bandit who murdered the king of Thebes in another country. He was one among many. Just as the search for the murderer of Laios turns from a band of men to the quest for the one man who did "crimes unnameable things," the pollution that infects Thebes proves to be a more terrible thing than it appears at first: it comes from a man who murdered his father. Here a gap opens up between appearance and reality. The only connection between these distant worlds is the "demonic" or inexplicable appearance of words like *mysos* and the "unnameable things" in the first *stasimon*.

The revulsion of nature provoked by the murder of a father by his son is expressed in a plague in which the fundamental continuity between generations is aborted. Fruits and grains harden in their protective sheaths. Children come stillborn from their mothers' wombs. A tradition known to Pausanias gives us a measure of the real cause of the Theban plague. At Potniai (a small town near Thebes) the drunken votaries of the god Dionysos kill his priest at a sacrifice. The city is immediately infected by a plague. Apollo is consulted for a cure. His response gives one of the two possibilities of the *Oedipus*: the stain of the priest's blood is cleansed by the ritual murder of a young man (*Guide to Greece*, IX 8.1). The Athenians in Sophocles' audience had reason to remember the pollution and curse that came from the murder of suppliants at the altars of the Furies just below the acropolis (Thucydides, I 126).

146 *bandits . . . not one man* All that is known about the murder of Laios comes from the sole survivor who not only spoke of bandits but was emphatic that one man did not do the deed. His insistence is significant for the play. The sole survivor of Oedipus' attack on Laios and his party is the household slave who was to expose Oedipus on Kithairon, but took pity on the baby. In the play, he is the only mortal besides Teiresias to know the truth about Oedipus and his life. When he fled from the scene of the murder he did not know that Laios was dead. But on his return to Thebes he learned that Laios had been killed and that Oedipus had taken his place as king of Thebes (992). We are not told that he recognized Oedipus as the child he saved, but the

fact that he insisted that Laios had been killed by bandits—not by one man alone—and his desire never to see Thebes again (996), speak for themselves. Sophocles gave his audience a sense of all that this shepherd knows well before his reluctant appearance.

156 *The intricate, hard song of the Sphinx*   Her song, and oracle (cf. 1530), is this:

> There is a creature that moves upon the earth
> on two feet, on four, and on three.
> He has one name, and of all the creatures that move
> upon the land, and through the bright air and sea,
> only this changes his condition. But when he
> walks with the most limbs to support him,
> he moves slowest and his limbs are weakest.

The answer to her riddle is Man; in Sophocles' play Oedipus is revealed as an infant on Kithairon, a man standing steady at the height of his power, and a blind exile who must walk upon the earth with a staff to support him and direct his way.

183-285 *Parodos*

196 *the turning season*   The Chorus envisage the possibility that the past is in control of the present—a possibility that is later rejected. See Introduction IV and the note to 669.

197-216 This prayer to three of the gods who protect or might protect Thebes bears a striking resemblance to the kind of cultic hymn that is a prayer based on precedent. The best example of this kind of appeal is Sappho's hymn to Aphrodite: "come to me now, if ever before you have heard and heeded my voice and prayer." "You saved me before" seems to lead nowhere, for the "black flame of suffering" (cf. 212) is very thin as a description of the tyranny of the Sphinx. Bernard Knox has argued that the only satisfactory way of grounding this reference is to see in it an allusion to the first of the plagues that wasted Athens (cf. Introduction V). The association of Ares and the plague in Sophocles is strange, and the best explanation of it seems to be historical, and to forge still another link between Thebes and Athens. The first outbreak of the plague in Athens occurred in the second year of Athens' war with Sparta (429 B.C.).

231 *the cold god of evening* is Hades, god of the dead, whose dwellings were thought to lie beyond the setting sun.

243 *the warm bright face of peace*   At the end of this ode, Oedipus is on stage. There is no better cue in what the Chorus say than this for his appearance.

252 *the two seas at the world's edge*   The Atlantic and the Black Sea or "Euxine" or sea "hospitable to strangers" by the Greek habit of euphemism which avoids provoking dangerous powers by naming them by their contraries.

277 *god whose name is our name*   So Thebes, the site of the oriental Dionysos' vindication of his claim to power over Greece, is called "Bacchic" (cf. Ajax 574 and 430).

286-635 First Episode

316 *the curse*   Oedipus describes his curse on the murderer of Laios as an epos— the word that describes the language that comes from Delphi (cf. 104). It is in fact prophetic, and it haunts the play (see the note to 591, and cf. 1055-1061).

366 *for every royal generation of Thebes*   In Sophocles' Greek, Oedipus gives the lineage of the kings of Thebes. His interest in the history of his adoptive city reveals his desire to sink down roots. When he has discovered his lineage, Oedipus no longer needs to qualify "as if he were my father" (361). And he is no longer interested in a family whose tree can be described as:

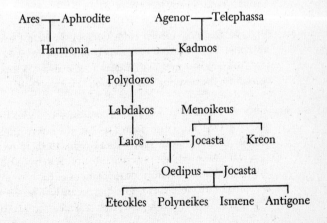

458 *You don't see how much alike we are*   The play of words is extremely subtle: Oedipus says of Teiresias that he is capable of provoking a rock. Teiresias replies by saying that Oedipus' anger, temper, or temperament is close to his own. Orge is the word on which all of this turns, and it is associated here with *phyᶜis*, origin or nature, literally, the "nature" of a rock. It would seem that Oedipus resembles Teiresias in a fixity of disposition. Teiresias has no choice but to know what he knows, and Oedipus has no choice, except for the decisive act of blinding himself, but to suffer what he suffers.

490 *Are you trying to make me say the word?*   The word that hangs on Teiresias' lips is phoneus, murderer—the word Oedipus responds to by the strong term "pain, hurt" (*pēmonaí*). In Greek, words were sticks and stones; see Introduction IV, and Lysias' speech *Against Theomnestos* (Speeches X and XL). The unspeakable words of Apollo's response to Oedipus, the language that describes the plot of the play itself, are oneide—bitter, hateful insults and the acts that provoke them (1036).

514-515 *You, you and your fate belong to Apollo*   Just the reverse of what a long manuscript tradition preserves. This tradition has Teiresias say: "I am not doomed to be ruined by you." The reasons for abandoning this tradition and shifting the reference to Oedipus are first the context: Oedipus speaks of Teiresias as incapable of harming him or anyone who has the power of sight. Teiresias answers by saying that he cannot in fact do any harm to Oedipus, nor can Kreon himself (518). The second consideration is simply that the reference to the ruin of Teiresias leads nowhere in the play, but "you and your fate belong to Apollo" leads directly to 1731-1738.

537 *stupid, untutored Oedipus* (mēden eidōs Oidípous)   Here Oedipus associates his name with the verb oída which means "I have seen" and therefore "I know"—a meaning Shelley rendered by Witfoot. The name also carries the meaning "Swollenfoot," cf. 1304-1308.

591 *your happiness an ember of pain*   Here Teiresias' words echo the precise language of Oedipus' curse (316-341), as they have already when the prophet tells Oedipus, "Never speak again to these men of Thebes" (476). These words are one guarantee of Teiresias' skill as a prophet and insight into the hidden configurations of the present, since he was not present to hear them. Oedipus, who had begun by addressing Teiresias as godlike and treating him as a man (cf. 412-414), is slow to

register the strange echoes of his own language in what Teiresias says; he is too absorbed in his concern for the human and the political. The realization of their meaning begins to come only later: "It is frightening—can the blind prophet see?" (979).

636-690 First *Stasimon*

669 *I know nothing about a feud*   The Chorus do not know how to react to the accusations Teiresias has made against Oedipus. Neither the present nor the future can give them the basis for understanding his words, and the past offers no help. Sophocles' Thebans know of no quarrel or feud (*neikos*) that involved either the sons of Labdakos or the son of Polybos. Translators usually reduce the sense of this language to: "I know of no trouble between Laios and Oedipus." But the Greek is disjunctive, and Laios and Oedipus are referred to by their patronymics. I have suggested (Introduction IV) that in Aeschylus' treatment of the history of the house of Laios in his tragic trilogy *Laios, Oedipus, Seven,* Sophocles had an answer at hand to the question of his Chorus. The plot of the *Seven,* like the plot of the *Oresteia,* is under the control of the past. What happens to Oedipus' sons is brought about by a father's curse and the disobedience of Laios—"an old breach of law, long since begotten" (in the translation of Hecht and Bacon, 940-941). The consequences of this breach work through three generations (743), in three waves (758-760). The intelligibility of this Aeschylean past is not a part of Sophocles' *Oedipus.*

675 *Zeus and Apollo know*   the gods who have shaped and guaranteed the plot of the *Oedipus,* are *xunetoi* and *eidotes,* literally, capable of putting things together, seeing and knowing. Finally these gods will reveal to men how the pieces in the puzzle of Oedipus' life fit together (1149-1151).

691-1104 Second Episode

814-816 *You won't change your mind*   In the MSS. this line is given to Oedipus and follows directly on "I'll believe you when you teach me the meaning of envy" (given to Kreon). The context demands that the order and attribution of the verses be reversed. It is Oedipus who must relent and believe what Kreon has said in his own defense (cf. 819, 849, 853 and *Ajax* 371). This rearrangement takes care of one problem in the text, but seems to create another by leaving a gap in the movement of thought between lines 814 and 816. Our translation reproduces in English what it is that Kreon responds to in Oedipus' threat. In the Greek it is Oedipus' use of the word envy (*phthonein*) which triggers Kreon's response: (Envy?) "Envy, you talk about envy. You don't even know what sense is" (*phronein*).

833 *petty personal bickering* Jocasta's entrance is the turning point of the *Oedipus*. From this moment on, the action of the play turns from the public to the private, from the search for the murderer of Laios to Oedipus' search for his origins.

845-848 By his oath, which is nearly incomprehensible to a modern audience, Kreon has put himself outside the sphere of the human and exposed himself to the terrible and ambiguous powers of the gods. He is *enágēs*. For the meaning of *agos*, see the note to 1852.

853-912 *Kommos* An antiphonal dirge between Oedipus on stage and the Chorus in the orchestra.

1028 *a future dark with torment* What Apollo revealed to Oedipus in answer to Oedipus' question about his birth involves one of the most terrible words in the Greek language (*patróktonos*, cf. 1566) and something so repellingly attractive that Greek had no generic word for it (it fills the silence at 1666). Apollo's predictions and the plot of the *Oedipus* center on acts that are called *oneíde* (cf. the note to 490). Oedipus' tormented thoughts about the life that awaits his daughters (1927-1942) give a modern audience some notion of how stinging Apollo's words were for Greeks who lived in a "shame culture" and spoke a language in which "to hear well or badly" meant to have a good or bad reputation.

1040 *near the crossroads you mentioned* Jocasta spoke of the place where roads join as the place of Laios' murder (716). Oedipus' memory is more precise.

1105-1158 Second *Stasimon*

1106 *let what I say be pure* The Chorus react to what Jocasta has said about the force of oracles (cf. 1145-1151). Jocasta will have even more shocking things to say just before Apollo's oracles are revealed as alive and true:

"oracles of the gods, where are you now!" (1197). And so will Oedipus (1217-1227). But Jocasta's deeds are those of a pious woman who recognizes in Oedipus' agitation the work of some god or demon (1159-1174). "Let all my acts be pure" is the Chorus' response to Oedipus' sudden fear that he has been polluted by the stain of Laios' blood (1062-1078).

1115 *arrogance insatiable pride* The Greek word for this is *hubris*—a going beyond limits. These lines, and the rest of this *stasimon*, have been taken to refer to Oedipus, to Jocasta, to Laios and his violent seduction of Chrysippos, the son of Pelops, or to a concept of empire and man in which Oedipus and the arrogance of imperial Athens come to be fused in one dramatic symbol. The desperate ingenuity and discordant variety in the interpretations of the meaning of this *stasimon* might itself prove to be a part of Sophocles' meaning, or point to it. Behind the image of the *tyrannos* the Chorus recall in its familiar features, there is some of the substance of the *Oedipus*. Oedipus has touched untouchable things (1139), and on the level of verbal ripples, the language of the Chorus seems to spread to Oedipus in the word "breeds" and the pointed references to feet and a fall (cf. Introduction IV). But what of the other details—the insatiable desires for forbidden things, the greed, the high-headed and high-handed contempt for justice and the gods? These are the marks of the *tyrannos*. This tragic costume is too big for Oedipus, and it comes from another age. It fits the Xerxes of Aeschylus' *Persians* and the Agamemnon of the *Oresteia* better than it does Oedipus (cf. *Agamemnon*, 367-384; 456-474; 527-532; 750-781; 905-911; 944-957).

In this *stasimon*, which is at the center of the play, Sophocles seems to turn to one possible explanation of Oedipus' tragedy, not because it can explain why Oedipus suffered what he suffered, but precisely because it cannot. By opening and closing the doors of his stage on the traditional figure of the *tyrannos*, Sophocles seems to assert that the action of the *Oedipus* is both autonomous and radically conditioned by forces that are beyond human understanding and human control. Neither the offenses of Laios nor the "tyrannical" actions of Oedipus explain the fate of Sophocles' hero. In this central ode, the Chorus respond to a moment in the discovery of the truth of Oedipus' life and fate. They are old men, wed to the past and limited and defined by the restraints and sentiments of a democratic *polis*. A measure of the incommensurability of their world and that of the Sophoclean hero is their evocation of the *tyrannos*. At the end of the play, this same Chorus can turn to the audience and point to Oedipus and intone: "Count no man happy until he is dead."

1148 *the temples at Olympia at Abai* The importance of these places is that they were both sites of oracles; Abai had an oracular sanctuary of Apollo and Olympia had an oracle of Zeus—the two gods who know the plot of the *Oedipus* (cf. 675, 963-964, 1731).

1159-1404 Third Episode

1168-1169 *Apollo . . . listen to my prayers* This is the cue for the entrance into the orchestra of the Messenger from Corinth. Jocasta prays for a "solution" to Oedipus' state acceptable to men and the gods. Her word is *lysis*. It means both a cleansing and an dénouement to the action of play (cf. Aristotle, *Poetics* 18).

1307 *That mark is the meaning of your name* Oedipus, Swollenfoot. For Oedipus, Witfoot, see the note to 537.

1376-1405 Third *Stasimon* This short, bouyant song is not a full choral *stasimon*. It closely resembles a dance form known as a *hypórchema*. Similar in mood and function is the exultant song to Pan in *Ajax* 693-718 which comes just before the news of Ajax's suicide. A good example of the *hypórchema* or "dance-song" is the vigorous Dionysiac song Pratinas composed for a chorus of satyrs (translated by A. M. Dale in her *Collected Papers* [Cambridge 1969] p. 168.)

1406-1501 Fourth Episode

1502-1572 Fourth *Stasimon*

1502 *man after man after man* ἰὼ γενεαὶ βροτῶν The beginning of this last choral song recalls inevitably Glaukos' reply to Diomedes in *Iliad* 6.145:

> why ask of my generation?
> As is the generation of leaves, so is that of humanity.
> The wind scatters the leaves on the ground, but the
> live timber
> burgeons with leaves again in the season of spring returning.
> So one generation of men will grow while another dies.
> (In the translation of Richmond Lattimore)

But significantly, and characteristically, the Sophoclean metaphor is that of light and darkness, appearance and the dark background, that both qualifies and defines the illusion of human happiness.

1573-1988 *Exodos*

1679-1680 *horror horror o what suffering men see* It could be that what the Chorus see is one of the "blind masks" that the lexicographer Pollux (early second century A.D.) treats briefly in his article on tragic masks (*Ono-masticon IV 141*). But the mask Oedipus wears does not resemble that of Teiresias, or a Phineus or a Thamyris. The artisan who made it would have had his model in the language of the messenger from the palace who describes Oedipus' self-mutilation.

1679-1776 *Kommos*

1730 *what demon lifted your hands* For the conception of character and responsibility behind this question, see Introduction II.

1852 *this cursed, naked, holy thing* This *agos*. In its distance from the Greek conception of the sacred, English must break the Greek word into its two, seemingly contradictory elements. For the Greek, the sacred is both holy and cursed, awful and dangerous, pure and polluted. By an oath earlier in the play Kreon had made himself *enáges*—that is, he had placed himself outside the human and exposed himself to the ambivalent powers of the divine (845-848). Jocasta had prayed to Apollo for a solution to Oedipus' troubled state that would be acceptable to the gods (a *lysin euagē* 1170), and this is the answer to her prayer: Oedipus has become an *agos*.

    The modern conception of the sacred does not possess the ambiguity of the ancient, and for a modern audience, the risks of Kreon's oath are impossible to appreciate. By penetrating the sphere of the sacred, Oedipus has acquired a power, a *menos*, that is fundamentally ambivalent. The Oedipus of the *Oedipus at Kolonos* represents a power that can work for either good or ill. In the grove of the Eumenides, the benevolent ones who are also Furies, Oedipus can become either benevolent (*eumenes*) or destructive (*dysmenes*), and his ambiguous and ambivalent power is at the center of the play. This same power is at the center of the last scene of the *Oedipus*.

    Like the plague, the elemental recoil and revulsion provoked by Oedipus' crimes in an expression of a deep sympathy between man and nature. Oedipus' crimes, and the perversion of the natural order they represent, expel him from Thebes and the world of man. The earlier images of expulsion and isolation, of Ares the god the gods would drive from heaven and the solitary bull cut off from the herd, come to center on Oedipus at the end of the play (283-285, 655, 1828-1834). Oedipus is *atheos*, abandoned by the gods (1774). He was driven from Corinth out of his fear that he would kill his father (*apoptolis*); and now he will be driven from Thebes.

The loathing felt for Oedipus goes beyond Thebes. As he stands blindly before the light of the sun, it becomes elemental. Like the Sinner Man the Holy Rollers sing of, Oedipus has no place in the natural world:

Run to the sea,
Sea'll be aboilin'—

Run to the moon
Moon'll be ableedin'.—

The theme is an old one. In Empedocles' *Purifications* (Diels-Kranz fragment B 115), the world of air, earth, fire, and water repels the godlike man who has polluted himself with bloodshed:

The force of the bright clear air drives him to the sea,
The sea spews him out onto land and earth,
The earth into the brilliant rays of the burning sun,
And the sun plunges him into the streams of bright, clear air.

1891 *no ordinary, natural death is mine* This strange language points enigmatically to the events of Sophocles' last treatment of the Oedipus story in *Oedipus at Colonus*. In his final prophetic denunciation, Teiresias had revealed Oedipus' fate (626-627):

rich and powerful now, he will be a beggar,
poking his way with a stick, feeling his way to a strange country.

At the end of the play, Oedipus' fate remains unclear. Thebes still awaits some word from Delphi. In *Oedipus at Colonus*, Oedipus' fate becomes as clear as an oracle can be. The "strange country" of Teiresias' prophecy is Athens where Oedipus seeks refuge and the "resting place" revealed by Apollo is the grove of the Furies near the shrine to the local hero Colonus in Sophocles' own *deme* or township (cf. 46, 84-95; cf. Euripides, *Phoenissae* 1705-1707).

1978 *O citizens of Thebes*   These final lines are intoned, not sung, by the Chorus as a whole. When the Chorus of Theban elders turn to an Athenian audience, the gradual fusion of Thebes and Athens is complete. They point to the figure of Oedipus on stage who is slowly led back into the palace. What they say has caused great unhappiness among those who admire Sophocles and his *Oedipus*. It is difficult not to agree that they are bathetic, but it is equally difficult to reject them. Euripides' Oedipus looks back on them at the end of the *Phoenician Women* (1757-1763). The judgment that these closing lines are "unworthy" of Sophocles is indisputable, if what this judgment means is that Sophocles would not have used them himself to sum up the meaning of his *Oedipus*. But the fact is that Sophocles does not speak through the Chorus; he speaks only through his *Oedipus* as a whole. What the final words of the *Oedipus* suggest is that there is an unbridgeable gap between the tragic hero on stage and the Chorus whose traditional wisdom cannot comprehend the fate of a hero like Oedipus (cf. *Women of Trachis*, 1-3, and *Ajax* 1428-1430). The Athenians who found them profound would have gone from the theater of Dionysos down to the seashore.

GLOSSARY

ABAI, a small site N.E. of Thebes, with an oracle of Apollo.

APOLLO, in this play the god of prophecy, light, and healing whose temple at Delphi (q.v.) is, through the inspired intermediary of his priestess (the Pythia, q.v.), the source of the prophecies that center on the family of Laios. He is called "Lycian"—an ambiguous epithet whose meaning suggests the "destroyer."

ARES, the god of war and uniquely in this play the god of plague.

ARTEMIS, a goddess associated with animals, mountains, and the hunt.

ATHENA, the virgin daughter of Zeus, goddess of intelligence, and the warrior protectress of Athens, and in the *Oedipus*, Thebes.

BACCHUS, or Dionysos, the god of wine and the ecstasy and liberation it produces. Thebes was the place where he vindicated his claim over Greece, hence it is called "Bacchic."

DAULIA, in Phocis (the region of Delphi), just off the road from Thebes to Delphi to the north.

DELPHI, in the mountains above the north coast of the gulf of Corinth; the site of the greatest prophetic shrine in Greece with its temple to Apollo and his oracle.

HADES, "the god of evening," the god of the dead.

HERMES, among other things, the god of herdsmen. Named in this play as the god who rules over Mt. Kyllene in N.E. Arcadia— the place of his birth.

JOCASTA, mother and wife of Oedipus.

KITHAIRON, a high, desolate mountain to the south of Thebes.

KREON, brother of Jocasta.

MEROPE, wife of Polybos (q.v.).

OEDIPUS, son of Laios and Jocasta, king of Thebes, and husband to Jocasta.

OLYMPIA, in Elis near the N.W. coast of the Peloponnesus, the greatest center for the worship of Olympian Zeus, mentioned because of its oracle of Zeus.

PAN, the Greek goat god, his lower quarters were those of a goat; from his thighs up he resembled a man. He is a god of music, lust, and the mountains.

PARNASSOS, the high mountain dominating Delphi (q.v.) to the N.E.

POLYBOS, king of Corinth, the adoptive father of the foundling Oedipus.

PYTHIA, the priestess of Apollo in his temple at Delphi. Possessed by the god, she pronounces or sings poetic responses to the questions of the visitors to the oracle of Apollo.

THE SPHINX, a demonic creature of three forms: she has the head of a woman, the body of a bird, and the hind quarters of a lion. Her riddle about a creature with three forms (first walking on four legs, then two, then three) was solved by Oedipus. Her name means the "strangler."

TEIRESIAS, a blind Theban prophet.

ZEUS, the father of Olympian gods, who in the *Oedipus* is associated with Apollo and prophecy as all-knowing.